AMERICAN CITIZENSHIP

THE TANNER LECTURES
ON HUMAN VALUES

D0169482

AMERICAN CITIZENSHIP

THE QUEST FOR INCLUSION

★

JUDITH N. SHKLAR

HARVARD UNIVERSITY PRESS

CAMBRIDGE, MASSACHUSETTS

LONDON, ENGLAND

Chapters 1 and 2 are based on material originally presented as part of the Tanner Lectures on Human Values, and are reprinted with permission of the University of Utah Press from *Tanner Lectures on Human Values*, vol. II, Salt Lake City. Copyright © 1990 by the University of Utah Press.

First Harvard University Press paperback edition, 1995

Library of Congress Cataloging-in-Publication Data
Shklar, Judith N.
American citizenship : the quest for inclusion / Judith N. Shklar.
p.   cm. — (The Tanner lectures on human values)
Includes index.
ISBN 0-674-02215-7 (cloth)
ISBN 0-674-02216-5 (pbk.)
1. Citizenship—United States.   I. Title.   II. Series.
JK1763.S48   1991
323.6'0973—dc20
90-35964
CIP

For
Michael Walzer

ACKNOWLEDGMENTS

These brief essays began as Tanner Lectures which I gave at the University of Utah in May 1989. I should like to thank all those I met there for their hospitality, the liveliness of their discussions, and the interest they showed in what I had to say. It was an altogether exhilarating experience.

As always I have been very fortunate in my friends, and as an author I know of few pleasures greater than being able to thank them for their help and encouragement. Benjamin Barber, Amy Gutmann, Stanley Hoffmann, Patrick Riley, Nancy Rosenblum, Michael Sandel, and Sidney Verba all read one or another version of these essays and gave me some very good advice, most of which I took. But George Kateb and Rogers Smith did more; they instructed me and made me change my mind about some of the questions that I discuss here. I am grateful to every one of them and hope that I can do as much for them eventually. Finally, there is a free and happy obligation of deep disagreement. This book is inscribed to Michael Walzer. We have argued about every subject of serious intellectual importance to both of us for decades without even wishing to alter each other's views, not least about citizenship. We may not even agree about the value of our conflicts, but as an inveterate liberal I prize them as much I cherish him as a friend.

CONTENTS

Introduction

I

ONE

VOTING

25

TWO

EARNING

63

Notes

105

Index

115

AMERICAN CITIZENSHIP

INTRODUCTION

THERE is no notion more central in politics than citizenship, and none more variable in history, or contested in theory. In America it has in principle always been democratic, but only in principle. From the first the most radical claims for freedom and political equality were played out in counterpoint to chattel slavery, the most extreme form of servitude, the consequences of which still haunt us. The equality of political rights, which is the first mark of American citizenship, was proclaimed in the accepted presence of its absolute denial. Its second mark, the overt rejection of hereditary privileges, was no easier to achieve in practice, and for the same reason. Slavery is an inherited condition. In these essays I shall try to show, however briefly, the enormous impact that not merely the institution of black chattel slavery but servitude as an integral part of a modern popular representative republic, dedicated to "the blessings of liberty," has had on the way Americans think about citizenship.

The dignity of work and of personal achievement, and the contempt for aristocratic idleness, have since Colonial times been an important part of American civic self-identification. The opportunity to work and to be paid an earned reward for one's labor was a social right, because it was a primary source of public respect. It was seen as such, however, not only because it was a defiant cultural and moral departure from the corrupt European past, but also because paid labor separated the free man from the slave. The value of political rights was enhanced for the same reason. The ballot has always been a certificate of full membership in society, and its value depends primarily on its capacity to confer a minimum of social dignity.

Under these conditions citizenship in America has never been just a matter of agency and empowerment, but also of social standing as well. I shun the word *status* because it has acquired a pejorative meaning; I shall speak of the standing of citizens instead. To be sure, standing is a vague notion, implying a sense of one's place in a hierarchical society, but most Americans appear to have a clear enough idea of what it means, and their relative social place, defined by income, occupation, and education, is of some importance to them. They also know that their concern for their social standing is not entirely compatible with their acknowledged democratic creed. Often they tend to resolve the conflict between conduct and ideology by assuring themselves that really there is less exclusiveness and status-consciousness than there used to be in the past.[1] Nevertheless, standing as a place in one of the higher or lower social strata and the egalitarian demand for "respect" are not easily reconciled. The claim that citizens of a democracy are entitled to respect unless they forfeit it by their own unacceptable actions is not a triviality. On the contrary, it is a deeply cherished belief, and to see just how important it has always been, one has to listen to those Americans who have been deprived of it through no fault of their own.

The significance of the two great emblems of public standing, the vote and the opportunity to earn, seems clearest to these excluded men and women. They have regarded voting and earning not just as the ability to promote their interests and to make money but as the attributes of an American citizen. And people who are not granted these marks of civic dignity feel dishonored, not just powerless and poor. They are also scorned by their fellow-citizens. The struggle for citizenship in America has, therefore, been overwhelmingly a demand for inclusion in the polity, an effort to break down excluding barriers to recognition, rather than an aspiration to civic participation as a deeply involving activity.

I do not intend to imply that citizenship as standing is the only meaning that the very idea of citizenship has in American history. Quite the contrary. The word *citizenship* has at least four quite distinct though related meanings, and what I have called standing is only one of these. Three equally significant meanings are citizenship as nationality, as active participation or "good" citizenship, and finally, ideal republican citizenship. These other ways of considering citizenship are so important that I want to make sure I do not give the impression of having ignored or neglected them.

In any modern state and especially in an immigrant

society, citizenship must always refer primarily to nationality. Citizenship as nationality is the legal recognition, both domestic and international, that a person is a member, native-born or naturalized, of a state. Such citizenship is not trivial. To be a stateless individual is one of the most dreadful political fates that can befall anyone in the modern world. And the possession of an American passport particularly is profoundly valued, especially by naturalized citizens. Few indeed are the new American citizens who have chosen to throw their naturalization papers away.

American citizenship as nationality has its own history of exclusions and inclusions, in which xenophobia, racism, religious bigotry, and fear of alien conspiracies have played their part. In the years before the Civil War the civic position of alien residents of the United States was, moreover, dependent upon the conflicting interests of the various states and of the federal government. Its history has, therefore, been extremely complicated. For instance, at one time Midwestern states were so starved for labor that they offered any alien white male the vote immediately upon declaring his intention eventually to become a citizen. At the same time the citizens of New England were contemplating ways and means to exclude their Irish neighbors from full citizenship.[2] The history of immigration and naturalization policies is not, however, my subject. It has its own ups and downs, but it is not the same as that of the exclusion of native-born Americans from citizenship. The two histories have their parallels, since both involve inclusion and exclusion, but there is a vast difference between discriminatory immigration laws and the enslavement of a people.

Citizenship as nationality is a legal condition; it does not refer to any specific political activity. Good citizenship as political participation, on the other hand, concentrates on political practices, and it applies to the people of a community who are consistently engaged in public affairs. The good democratic citizen is a political agent who takes part regularly in politics locally and nationally, not just on primary and election day. Active citizens keep informed and speak out against public measures that they regard as unjust, unwise, or just too expensive. They also openly support policies that they regard as just and prudent. Although they do not refrain from pursuing their own and their reference group's interests, they try to weigh the claims of other people impartially and listen carefully to their arguments. They are public meeting–goers and joiners of voluntary organizations who discuss and deliberate with others about the policies that will affect them all, and who serve their country not only as taxpayers and occasional soldiers, but by having a considered notion of the public good that they genuinely take to heart. The good citizen is a patriot.

Such active citizenship often shades over into bordering private spheres. The phrase *good citizen* is now very commonly used to refer to people who behave well on the job and in their immediate neighborhood. Whistle-blowing not only on corrupt officials but on company management, or just being alert to the injustices of daily life, are normally spoken of as acts of good citizenship. University departments, for instance, routinely speak of some of their members as good citizens, by which they mean that they do their share of chores such as sitting on dull committees, teaching elementary courses, and attending meetings rather than just doing what is often called "their own work." The same is said of people who do their best for their immediate surroundings, through activities like keeping the local playground reasonably clean and safe, attending PTA meetings, and shoveling the snow off their part of the sidewalk in winter. These are in fact what we might well call decent people, because they have a sense of obligation to the social environment that they share immediately with their occupational or local neighbors. It is a use of the word *citizenship* that has no policy implications, but it is an internalized part of a democratic order that relies on the self-direction and responsibility of its citizens rather than on their mere obedience. Whether in private or in public, the good citizen does something to support democratic habits and the constitutional order.

Good citizenship should not be confused with what is usually meant by goodness. We have known since Aristotle that a good citizen is not the same as a good man.[3] Good citizens fulfill the demands of their polity, and they are no better and no worse as citizens than the laws that they frame and obey. They support the public good as it is defined by their constitution and its fundamental ethos. The good person and the good citizen could only be identical in a perfect state, and even then only if we accept the notion that civic virtue, manly rectitude as the term implies, is the best human character. With that exception the possibility of tension between personal morality and citizenship is always possible and even likely, and there are, of course, regimes so terrible that good people are bound to be bad citizens there, but America has never been quite that bad. It was only half a despotism, part free, part slave. Surely the American citizens who performed all their civic obligations under a constitution that sanctioned slavery were not bad citizens; they lived up to the requirements of their half-free society. This was as true of those among them who were serious and consistent abolitionists as of those who, like Lincoln, acted on the belief that abolition would take a long time and who were not ready to risk a war for the sake of a population that they regarded as inferior, though they would fight for the preservation of Union. Neither they nor we are either perfect citizens or good human beings. Many Americans, however, have been and are good enough citizens of the republic as it was, is, and might be.

Historically the trouble has not been that Americans claimed that one had to be morally good to be a citizen. On the contrary, women particularly were said to be good more frequently than men, but they were not fit to be citizens. In this respect the differences between the good person and the good citizen have been fully understood from the first. What renders any group or individual unfit for citizenship is economic dependence, race, and gender, which are all socially created or hereditary conditions. Such rules would seem to imply a political system that is in no sense democratic or liberal, but it was never that simple, because Americans have lived with extreme contradictions for most of their history by being dedicated to political equality as well as to its complete rejection.

These attitudes to citizenship were evidently deeply entrenched in the institutional and ideological structure of the United States, and they have left their traces amid the many changes of the present century. And indeed citizenship cannot be discussed apart from its political setting, not only because of Aristotle's distinction between good men and good citizens but also because of his equally pertinent observation that citizenship is more changeable than and quite distinct from a person's or a group's physical character.[4] An oligarchic coup d'état can transform the citizens of a democracy into quite different political animals, for example. In spite of nationalist rhetoric, national character, whatever it may mean, does not define citizenship. The citizens of the Third, Fourth, and Fifth French Republics were not at all like those of the Vichy regime, but they were physically the same Frenchmen, and one need hardly mention the history of German citizenship in the present century to see the point. More important here is the fact that American citizenship has also been transformed in the course of constitutional, institutional, demographic, and international changes, of which the nationalization and expansion of the functions of government and several constitutional amendments are merely the most obvious and fundamental.

If these essays have any polemical purpose, it is not only to join those scholars who have belatedly come to recognize the part that slavery has played in our history. Important as that rethinking of our past is, I also want to remind political theorists that citizenship is not a notion that can be discussed intelligibly in a static and empty social space. Whatever the ideological gratifications that the mnemonic evocation of an original and pure citizenry may have, it is unconvincing and ultimately an uninteresting flight from politics if it disregards the history and present actualities of our institutions. Citizenship has changed over the years, and political theorists who ignore the best current history and political science cannot expect to have anything very significant to contribute to our political self-understanding.[5] They stand in acute danger of theorizing about nothing at all except their own uneasiness in a society they have made very little effort to comprehend. Neither Supreme Court opinions, which at times serve to structure our public debates, nor the writings of other philosophers, however distinguished, can act as a substitute for a genuinely historical and politically informed understanding of what citizenship has been and now is in America.[6]

The reasons for imagining that American citizenship has never altered are curious. It may well be that because America's basic institutions seem to have changed so little since 1787, we often discuss citizenship as if it existed in an institutional deep freeze. The unchanging permanence of the political structure is simply being taken for granted because of its formal continuity, even by those who do remember the significance of the constitutional amendments that followed the Civil War. Moreover, the longevity of the ideology that goes under the entirely appropriate name of "the American Dream" is indeed an extraordinary phenomenon.[7] Its roots lie far back in the first decades of the last century, and I hope to explore them in these essays. The endurance of much of the original Constitution and of the faith in its promise does not, however, justify the assumption that nothing significant has happened to American citizenship since the eighteenth century. To be sure, like the ancient Romans, we too may find the stability of authority and the gratifying support of tradition in acts of ancestor worship.[8] Nothing, however, would have mortified the actual founders of the republic more deeply. Every page of *The Federalist Papers* is a call to the people of America to take its fate into its own hands and to fashion its institutions in the light of the best political science of the present, rather than to look timidly to the past. The good citizen of today can do no less.

There has always been in addition to nationality and good citizenship a vision of the ideal citizen that has haunted especially those who have dreams about mythical Athens or Sparta. Ordinary active or good citizens are certainly not ideal or perfect citizens; they just try to live up to the recognized demands of a representative democracy. Ideal republican patriots are quite different. They have no serious interests apart from public activity; they live in and for the forum. These perfected citizens are sometimes thought to be healthier and more fulfilled than people who are indifferent to politics, but there is little medical proof of such a proposition. Many people might not thrive on uninterrupted political engagement. Since the turn of the century it has, more relevantly, been argued that the best cure for the faults of democratic government is more, not less, democracy. The steady movement toward more direct government by means of referenda, recalls, and initiatives has been based on this assumption, with rather uncertain results.[9] These opportunities for political expression have not particularly impressed the advocates of truly participatory democracy because they are still ways of voting on measures without intensely experienced deliberative involvement.

In the ideal republic the virtuous citizen would be constantly and directly involved in ruling as well as in being ruled. What is meant by "virtue" is of course not altogether clear, but it is more than the merely active citizen now displays. At the very least, perfect citizens will pursue the public good with single-minded devotion and will do so in a direct rather than in a representative democracy. They are, of course, members of a republic unlike the United States as it now is, ever has been, or is ever likely to be in any imaginable future. Their function is to act as a critical reflection upon imperfect democracy and the lack of zeal that most of us bring to our public life. One may well doubt their effectiveness.

The great classics of modern political theory have certainly followed Aristotle in emphasizing that it is the constitution that defines good citizenship, not an ideal individual. Even Rousseau, who is the inventor of the modern model of the perfect citizen in the ideal democratic republic, understood this perfectly well. Montesquieu had instructed him no less than many American readers. They all knew that the good citizen of their extended modern republic would not be like the virtuous Romans, who had no personal identity at all apart from their citizenship. Good citizenship simply is not separable from the sort of society in which it functions. The call for perfect republican virtue itself is persuasive only if it is placed within the full context of a perfect democracy, radically different from the modern representative republic.[10] There is very little evidence to show that there are many Americans who contemplate such transformative politics with interest, let alone enthusiasm. The paradox of an ideal democratic citizenship that has no appeal to the people it is supposed to favor is not without irony.

Neither the defense nor the reform of contemporary American citizenship has much to gain from utopian republicanism or from nostalgic evocations of either the anti-federalists or their successful opponents. The good citizen of their age is no longer a model for us. We are not now and never were the inhabitants of sparsely populated, agrarian, homogeneous little states that only an anti-federalist with a vivid imagination could ever have compared to an ancient polis. And our pluralistic ethnic and interest-group politics do not resemble those that Madison represented when he sanctioned the "federal ratio" and factions. Such uninterrupted leaps from the beginning to the present have the obvious effect of distorting our actual situation and of giving us a false impression of sameness and indeed of vacuity.[11]

America has not marched single file down a single straight liberal highway as both the lamenters and the celebrators of its political life have claimed, either in despair or in complacency.[12] What has been continuous is a series of conflicts arising from enduring anti-liberal dispositions that have regularly asserted themselves, often very successfully, against the promise of equal political rights contained in the Declaration of Independence and its successors, the three Civil War amendments. It is because slavery, racism, nativism, and sexism, often institutionalized in exclusionary and discriminatory laws and practices, have been and still are arrayed against the officially accepted claims of equal citizenship that there is a real pattern to be discerned in the tortuous development of American ideas of citizenship. If there is permanence here, it is one of lasting conflicting claims, and it is to these that the following essays are devoted.

In concentrating upon citizenship as standing I do not underestimate the importance of nationality, nor have I forgotten how ungenerous and bigoted immigration and naturalization policies have often been, but I think that their effects and defects pale before the history of slavery and its impact upon our public attitudes. Nor do I wish to imply that efforts to teach and praise good citizenship are unimportant; nothing could be more necessary to maintain democracy. However, democratic ideology was also implicated in exclusions from citizenship. Political passivity was not the only flaw in this case by any means. These essays are meant to recall that the disenfranchised and the excluded were members of a professedly democratic society that was actively and purposefully false to its own vaunted principles by refusing to accept these people or to recognize their right to be voters and free laborers. As slaves they were less than subjects of any modern state; as black freedmen and women they were at best no more than that. They were mere subjects, however, not in an absolute monarchy but in a constitutional democracy that certainly offered more to everyone else, and that refused to recognize how very far it was from realizing the "blessings of liberty." In truth, from the nation's beginnings as an independent republic, Americans were torn by "glaring inconsistencies between their professed principles of citizenship and their deep-seated desire to exclude certain groups permanently from the privileges of membership."[13] These tensions constitute the real history of its citizens.

One way to undertake a historically rich inquiry into American citizenship is therefore to investigate what citizenship has meant to those women and men who have been denied all or some of its attributes, and who ardently wanted to be full citizens. Their voices not only put the question of citizenship on the public agenda from the Revolution to the present; they also defined what was unique about American citizenship: voting and earning. Because exclusion was so much more common and so much easier than inclusiveness, citizenship was, moreover, always something that required prolonged struggle, and this also has molded its character. Citizenship so gained lost much of its urgency once it was attained. The years of denial have left their paradoxical marks upon this constitutional right.

The American Constitution does not mention citizenship at all until the Fourteenth Amendment, but Americans had quite clear ideas about what the social meaning of citizenship was, and when they were denied it, they protested. From the first they defined their standing as citizens very negatively, by distinguishing themselves from their inferiors, especially from slaves and occasionally from women. As long as the question of qualifications for voting was unsettled, even white males had grounds for uneasiness. Vermont and the newer Western states had no property qualifications, but poor white males in all the other states had to struggle for the vote, often for a long time. Massachusetts was one of the last to grant the vote to all of its males, with town meetings particularly reluctant to drop property requirements for voting altogether.[14] Only one thing was absolutely clear to everyone who used the word *citizen* in any of these early disputes about the vote: no slave was a citizen. Even before Justice Taney announced that no black person had any rights that white people needed to respect, black chattel slavery stood at the opposite social pole from full citizenship and so defined it. The importance of what I call citizenship as standing emerges out of this basic fact of our political history. The value of citizenship was derived primarily from its denial to slaves, to some white men, and to all women.

In the four great expansions of the suffrage, slavery was always a presence in the language of political argument. The Colonists rebelling against English rule, the white males disenfranchised by property and tax qualifications, the freedmen after the Civil War, and finally women all protested that they were reduced to the level of slaves if they did not have the vote and equal representation. The memory of servitude was, moreover, very much in the minds of the Southern black citizens who had to go to the courts in recent years to achieve their voting rights. In the case of all these claimants, except the freedmen, this amounted to some exaggeration, of course. However, where slavery is not just a figure of speech or a chapter in one's ancient history textbook but is an integral social institution, it is necessarily a threat. To be less than a full citizen is at the very least to approach the dreaded condition of a slave. To be a second-class citizen is to suffer derogation and the loss of respectable standing. It also has meant being ruled by others, if not wholly as the slave was, at least more so than free male citizens were—in the case of women a great deal more so.

The native-born Americans who fought for the same rights as the already enfranchised were engaged in the primordial struggle for recognition, in this case of their standing as republican citizens. Poor militia-men wanted to be citizen-soldiers, not mercenaries. Freedmen wanted their emancipation confirmed, especially those among them who had fought in the Civil War. Women were not prepared to remain confined to domesticity and a form of citizenship less complete than that of their fathers, brothers, husbands, and sons. What gave citizenship as standing its historical significance is not that it was denied for so long to so many, but that this exclusion occurred in a republic that was overtly committed to political equality, and whose citizens believed that theirs was a free and fair society.

Nothing, however, reveals the centrality of standing in these four episodes of suffrage reform more clearly than the attitudes of teenagers who had no reason to feel demeaned when they did not have the right to vote until they reached the age of twenty-one.

When there is no standing involved, the franchise is simply not valued. The Twenty-sixth Amendment was not sought by and was of no interest whatever to the eighteen-year-olds to whom it granted the vote. The purported beneficiaries of the amendment had not asked for it, nor did they rejoice in its passage. Many of them were not politically passive—they were protesting against the Vietnam war at the time when they were granted the vote—but the amendment was of no great concern to them. Introduced first as a legislative measure in the Senate, against the reasonable objections of civil rights advocates, it became a constitutional amendment only because the Supreme Court limited its constitutionality to federal elections. To avoid chaotic registration requirements in the states, the amendment was passed in less than three months, the least time ever spent on an amendment.[15] It was not seriously discussed at any time. A frivolous exercise, it was based on a complete misunderstanding of the value of enfranchisement.

Being young is, of course, not a permanent physical or social condition, and in a society that worships youth it is anything but degrading. In 1971 few youths were as interested in being citizen-soldiers as they were in avoiding the draft. So the right to vote was thrust upon them without in any way improving their standing or adding anything to their social position. On the contrary, in youth freedom means having fewer responsibilities than adults do. What this last extension of the franchise shows is that the vote gains its value from the standing that it confers. The utter indifference of the young stands in stark contrast to the intensity with which blacks and women, only too fixed in their physical and social condition, have fought for the vote and for their political standing.

The right to earn has a history parallel to that of the suffrage. Slaves certainly labor, but they are kept and are not paid a wage for their work. For some women who had no choice but to be homemakers the similarity was apparent, although it was clearly an overstatement to compare them to slaves. It was an analogy that was, however, deeply felt, even though it was not always politically opportune. It backfired in some cases for exactly the same reasons that it appealed in others. Many a wife and mother neither feels enslaved nor wants to be compared to a slave, a frightening condition that she cannot and does not wish to identify with her own. The suffrage movement was not universally supported by American women, a fair number of whom were content with their existing condition, disliked any radical social change, and, worst of all, feared that they would lose the support of their husbands and other male family members if they left their "proper sphere." Others, far more radical, considered the suffrage movement irrelevant to the more pressing needs of working women for protective labor legislation and family assistance. They could see no reason why they should be compared to slaves.[16] It seemed an insult, because slavery meant degradation. The Equal Rights Amendment was to meet a similar response in a number of instances. Significantly, it is the imputation of slavery, the very word *slave* when applied to homemakers, that arouses the deepest resentment on the part of conservative female opponents of the ERA.[17] There is nothing surprising in such a reaction. The reason why some women want to secure their rights is that they fear being second-class citizens, a mere step up from slavery. Women who do not want to alter their present standing are bitterly angered by such a comparison because they feel degraded by being likened to slaves. In either case the dreaded memory still lingers.

No black leader ever seems to have expressed a comparable hostility to the right to vote, but some were willing to postpone it in the interest of economic advancement and of the capacity and opportunity to earn. Booker Washington certainly never gave up the aspiration for eventual political rights for black Americans, but he was not alone in the age of energy and economic expansion to think that productive work and wealth were socially more significant.[18] The sense that conditions of work defined a person more than political rights also came to affect the outlook of Northern white workers, who since the years before the Civil War complained of being reduced to wage-slavery.

The fear of sinking into slavery was certainly real enough among the new factory workers, not least because Southern propagandists assured them that they were worse off than black chattel slaves. In part the cry

of "wage-slavery" was also a protest against the abolitionists, who seemed to be indifferent to the sufferings
of the white workers in their midst as they concen-
trated on the black slaves in the South.[19] The leading
abolitionists rejected the comparison, but after emancipation both William Lloyd Garrison and Wendell
Phillips certainly lent their support to the labor movement's drive for shorter hours and more tolerable conditions. They did so explicitly for the same reasons
that had earlier moved them to oppose slavery in the
South.[20]

Northern free workers, of course, knew that they
were not slaves and were not interested in becoming
real ones, for all the talk about the good life enjoyed
by black slaves on Southern plantations. They were,
however, experiencing a decided decline in independence and income as a result of massive immigration
and the introduction of factory work. When these
workers became just another factor in the process of
production, they came to see the specter of slavery.
They knew that their contracts were not conditions of
employment which they had freely accepted; they had
given their "*assent* but do not *consent, they submit but
do not agree,*" as one labor leader put it.[21] To call this a
free contract was as false as to say that it was enslavement. What they did argue was that they were no
longer the independent republican citizens that they
had been before they had to work for wages. Not just
income but independence was at stake.

After the Civil War, as workers began to unionize to

improve their working lives and with slavery abolished, one might expect the old fears to subside, but
they did not. Unions could and did do much to improve working life, but they could not prevent unemployment, and when one is unemployed one loses
one's standing in America. During the Great Depression the unemployed workers of America still regarded both their lack of income and their need to rely
on some form of assistance as a shameful loss of independence and beneath the dignity of a citizen. By now
unemployment is recognized as a social misfortune
rather than a disgrace, but long-term welfare dependence is not seen in that light at all. To be on welfare is
to lose one's independence and to be treated as less
than a full member of society. In effect, the people who
belong to the under-class are not quite citizens.

The two following essays cannot pretend to be an
exhaustive account of American citizenship. They are
reflections upon its history, about which much more
could and should be said. I have only tried to recall
something that has too often been neglected by historians of American political thought: the enduring impact of slavery not merely on black Americans and on
the Civil War generation generally, but also on the
imagination and fears of those who were neither
threatened by enslavement nor deeply and actively
opposed to it. The word *slavery* used to express fears
of oppression in a country where slaves are constantly
before one's eyes or at least are a living presence has a
different meaning from its use as merely a figure of

speech. Rebellious Europeans might cry out that they were enslaved, but they had never seen the real thing. Americans lived with it in pain, guilt, fear, and hatred. It was a profound experience and was to put its mark on the most basic institution of our public life, American citizenship.

CHAPTER ONE

VOTING

O F COURSE I know how illusory would be the belief that my vote determined anything; but nevertheless when I go to the polls I have a satisfaction in the sense that we are all engaged in a common venture," Judge Learned Hand once said.[1] Many of us share his emotions as we go to the voting booth. We are taking part in a serious and personally significant ritual. When we remember them, we feel sorry for the many people in other parts of the world who are not permitted to cast ballots. We know, moreover, that voting is central to our entire system of government. The simple act of voting is the ground upon which the edifice of elective government rests ultimately. But almost half of the American electorate does not bother to vote at all.

There is nothing new either about the failure to vote or about the laments that this delinquency inspires. Alexander Hamilton already noted "the alarming in-difference discoverable in the exercise of so invaluable a privilege," and predictably blamed the voters rather than the difficulties of getting to the polls.[2] Through-out the present century, the low turnout at the polls has particularly worried political scientists. It seems so "abnormal," so wrong, to ignore elections when so much depends upon their outcome.[3] From the first to the latest studies of non-voting, political scientists have also argued about the causes of this distressing American political conduct. Some believe that obstructive registration laws are at fault, or the inaccessibility of the polls, as Hamilton's opponents believed.[4] Others think that voting is a meaningless gesture for the many people who feel that the political system is indifferent to their concerns and who can see no point in taking part in a ritual that has no bearing on their lives. In the absence of any consequences, why should they bestir themselves?

For the voters, on the other hand, voting is "an affirmation of belonging" rather than the exercise of a right.[5] For educated people especially, "the most important benefit of voting . . . is expressive rather than instrumental: a feeling that one has done one's duty to society . . . and to oneself."[6] There is no particular reason why both indifference and hindrances to voting should not contribute to poor voter turnout. It is, however, always far more difficult to explain why something does not happen or why someone does not act than to account for events that have occurred. The reasons for investigating non-events at all are also often complex. We want to know why a group or individuals did not perform some given actions because we think that they ought to have done so. The surprise is not necessarily due to an unfulfilled prediction; it just as often expresses moral disappointment. The Marxist ink that has been spilled over the refusal of American workers to behave as the doctrine prescribed is not just a matter of scientific puzzlement. These writers are plainly angry. It is so with non-voting as well. If voting were not an ethical expectation as well as a social norm, political observers would probably care far less about it.

I do not know why so many Americans choose not to vote. In all likelihood there are a good many reasons for it. It is, however, something that should concern us, because symbolic satisfactions in the affirmation of citizenship are not trivial in the light of our history. When one considers how passionately disenfranchised American men and women have for two centuries yearned and struggled for the suffrage, it seems deplorable that their more fortunate successors should care so little for it. Nevertheless, we should perhaps not be as astonished as we often are. It was the denial of the suffrage to large groups of Americans that made the right to vote such a mark of social standing. To be refused the right was to be almost a slave, but once one possessed the right, it conferred no other personal advantages. Not the exercise, only the right, signified deeply. Without the right one was less than a citizen. Once the right was achieved, it had fulfilled its function in distancing the citizen from his inferiors, especially slaves and women. To be a voter was thus as much a condition as a call to action, and those who do vote today are still celebrating the civic estate for which so many generations of excluded men and women have fought so energetically.

What did citizenship mean to disenfranchised and dependent men and women? Only by considering their aspirations for public standing, personal independence, and shared political rights can one hope to develop a historically realistic account of American citizenship and its meaning. Even if it does not correspond to the various idealized versions of civic virtue, it may still claim our respect. These people fought for American rights, after all. In emphasizing their political hopes and efforts I may well appear to be overemphasizing the unique character of American citizenship, but I do not intend to stress what is often called "American exceptionalism." The right to vote and to be represented has been ardently pursued by people all over the world, but the relations between castes, classes, nationalities, and religions have made every one of these political struggles "exceptional," in the sense of their being different from one another. Here I mean to reflect upon the peculiarity of a democracy that has had to struggle not merely with a distant and inegalitarian European past, but also with its own infinitely more despotic institutions and beliefs.

The tension between an acknowledged ideology of equal political rights and a deep and common desire to exclude and reject large groups of human beings from citizenship has marked every stage of the history of American democracy. And it was this juxtaposition of slavery and constitutional democracy, above all else, that set America apart from other modern states. It is a difference that emerges at once when one reviews the history of ideas of citizenship in general.

Modern democratic citizenship was itself a new departure in political thinking, but political equality so intimately entwined with slavery as it was in America was doubly complicated. Nor has it, perhaps, been fully acknowledged or known. To be sure, the most famous of all accounts of citizenship, Aristotle's, was developed for a slave society, but it was hardly democratic in character or intent. After dismissing mere birth and residence as inadequate, he defined citizenship as ruling and being ruled. Only very few citizens can be said to be fit for such activities, or for the perfect education that is the true end of politics. This is a highly exclusive definition, for ideally only men who have the material means and personal breeding for leisure can achieve such citizenship. Women and slaves exist exclusively to serve them domestically. Moreover, since most forms of work are defiling, no one who labors can be fit for civic functions. Only the free and well-born can be genuine citizens, even if all the rest are not actually enslaved.

This is citizenship for members of a master-class who feel a real affinity for one another, and who can spend their time together discussing the great matters of policy, especially war, peace, and alliances, as well as domestic expenditures for these and other great public enterprises. Aristotelian citizenship is a mixture of character building and public activity among well-bred gentlemen with plenty of free time.[7] It is an ideal that has enchanted the admirers of Athens through the ages, not least those Americans who propose direct participatory democracy to us, forgetting just how exclusive educative citizenship on the Aristotelian model has to be, with its premium on cohesion among the fully active citizenry.[8] Much as it has excited the intellectual imagination, the concept of the Aristotelian citizen as ruler has not really had much bearing on Americans, since even its slave-owners professed far more individualistic and egalitarian values.

The enduring appeal of the Aristotelian vision of participatory aristocracy is in its account of the practice of citizenship and the importance of public activity in the daily lives of the citizens. It is not claimed that the distribution of citizenship was democratic, since the vast majority of persons so governed were excluded from all public activity or enslaved, but that the privileged enjoyed a perfect form of democratic activity. Disenfranchised Americans have not demanded this sort of citizenship. They have asked for something quite different, that citizenship be equally distributed, so that their standing might also be recognized and their interests be defended and promoted. The call for a classical participatory democracy may, therefore, be far from democratic, because it does not correspond to the aspirations of most Americans now and has never done so in the past. More often than not, the urge to play a part in the public sphere has led Americans to join voluntary organizations which promote some policy or cause that concerns them directly.

Quite different and far more significant for America than memories of ancient Athens is the figure of the citizen-soldier. Machiavelli has been rightly recognized as the most perfect modern defender of this ideal. His ideal citizen is a model of patriotic virtue, possessed of all the military qualities of readiness to fight and to sacrifice his personal interests for the sake of the military glory of his native land. Avarice and those gentler character traits derided as peculiarly feminine are excoriated as corrupt, precisely because they interfere with the true vocation of the citizen, military readiness and devotion to glory. To that end there must be good laws as well as good arms, and the virtuous citizen can be expected to support both, unlike the privileged classes, who tend naturally to self-oriented corruption.[9]

In every war young Americans came to harbor some of these sentiments, and asked whether men good enough to serve their country in war were not also fit to be full citizens. Indeed, were they not better able to perform the duties of citizenship than those who had not displayed comparable military valor? For many Americans the virtuous soldier was the man most fit to be a citizen of a genuinely republican order. This, however, was not a universally shared notion of civic virtue, and indeed, many Americans have always rejected the assumption that citizens had to prove their virtue in order to vote. Rights do not depend on it.

Nothing could be more remote from these essentially active forms of citizenship than the notion of the citizen as a loyal subject. Bodin and Hobbes were not just apologists for monarchical absolutism but designers of a political order that was meant to fulfill the most immediate needs of ordinary people: minimal security against conquest, civil war, anarchy, and private violence. The subject renounces all pretensions to legislative authority and in return receives security and even prosperity. According to Hobbes, this state of affairs was contractually established by rational men, and, in any case, it must be what people always want above all else and can achieve if they understand the causes and consequences of lawlessness. Absolute monarchs are no threat to ordinary people; even a Nero only destroyed the courtiers around him. Sovereignty is a matter of making and enforcing laws, and citizenship is at its height when subjects understand why they should obey them and do so invariably unless their lives are threatened, at which point they cease to be subjects. Until that extreme moment, subject-citizens are in one respect alike and equal: all are subjects to a sovereign.[10]

Consent need not play a significant part in the exercise of sovereignty. In Bodin's more conventional view, being a subject is natural and can be very inclusive. It comes to the sons of the natives born in a given state, and it can also be acquired by "naturalization," an imitation of nature, presumably, in which consent replaces the accident of birth. Bodin's citizen is "a free subject holding of the sovereignty of another man." It is, however, not an attribute merely of residence; what counts is being "under the power of another's command." Aristotle's definition was, in Bodin's view, "lame and defective" because ruling is a function of princes, while citizens are marked by the enjoyment of legally granted rights and privileges. There is a hint that a fair trial is one of them, but the freedom to leave the country is not. The natural citizen-subject owes the sovereign obedience; the latter owes him "tuition, justice and defense." The citizen is a protected subject. Man and citizen are identical; no special qualities distinguish the latter. He is a taxpayer. No moral qualities, whether natural or learned, are required. That makes exclusion and inclusion entirely a matter of law. Less philosophical than Hobbes, Bodin can claim to be the real inventor of the modern state and its limited but essentially equal and inclusive notion of citizenship.[11] To be sure, in the early modern state subjects were equal only before the sovereign, and vast inequalities of caste, political standing, power, and wealth prevailed. With the decline of monarchical sovereignty, however, the egalitarian implications of Hobbes's and Bodin's doctrine became evident and were played out, especially in France.

In America, however, which had never been an absolute monarchy, the notion of the citizen as a mere subject was reserved for free blacks, until the *Dred Scott* decision deprived them of even that standing. As one North Carolina judge put it in 1835, "the term 'citizen' as understood in our law, is precisely analogous to the term *subject* in common law . . . he who before was a 'subject of the king' is now 'a citizen of the state.' " A freedman might therefore be a citizen-subject, in this view, but "the possession of political power is not essential to constitute a citizen" so defined. Freedmen need not be admitted "into political partnership," the Pennsylvania Supreme Court agreed some years later, even if they were citizens of the state.[12]

To use the word *citizen* to describe a mere subject is offensive no less to democratic theory than to its practice, and it was among Rousseau's merits to have said so. Nevertheless, much as he excoriated them, Rousseau, the most coherent theorist of democratic citizenship, owed a lot to Hobbes and Bodin. His republican citizen is certainly not one who rules. The magistrates govern him, but he does take part in legislation, and thus he is both a member of the sovereign and a subject. By entering into a morally transforming contract, he becomes fit both to make and maintain the rules that set the conditions of citizenship, and that liberate him from personal dependence on other people. Not everyone can meet these stringent qualifications for citizenship. Women must certainly be excluded, because they are psychologically too powerful and too domineering to be allowed to share political authority. Nevertheless, Rousseau's picture of a perfect citizen is of a woman, a Spartan mother who rushes to give thanks for victory in a battle in which all her sons were killed. To achieve such a character clearly requires incessant education and reinforcement, and that is just what Rousseau envisaged.

When men become citizens, they not only acquire legally protected property but also a public conscience, a general will, which must often be at odds with the partial, personal will. And since republican citizenship is so entirely dependent on states of mind, it must both condition the beliefs of citizens and reject men who profess uncivil religious opinions. Xenophobia is helpful, while all manifestations of intellectuality are to be avoided in a society of peasant-patriots. Excessive differences in wealth invite dependence of the rich on the services of the poor and of poor on the favors of the rich. This citizen, unlike Hobbes's and Bodin's subject, expects more than mere tranquillity; he demands legally secured independence and equality of political rights. As one "who shares in the sovereign power," he cannot be represented but must act for himself in legislating, but he does so not as a discrete individual only, but also as a conscious member of the collective body of citizens. And when he fails to obey the laws he has given himself, he is only "forced to be free," even in receiving capital punishment, since it is no more than a legal requirement which he agreed to impose on all citizens alike. The lawbreaking citizen is really a traitor.

In a republic the citizen may participate in electing magistrates, but Rousseau was ready to see that this right was diluted as it had been in Rome, by voice voting in tribal assemblies. In a perfect democracy, the lot would do. These provisions are all entirely compatible with exclusion on grounds of moral deficiency and lack of civic stamina. In Rousseau's plan for Corsica only quite mature, land-owning males who had fathered at least two children could qualify.[13] This indeed is citizenship for the virtuous, and in the rhetoric of the anti-federalists it certainly found a place in eighteenth-century American politics, and it still has its admirers among participatory democrats.[14] Moreover, as a voting legislator Rousseau's sovereign citizen clearly must play a part in any theory of democracy, even if Americans have never been prepared to undertake the radical scheme of constant education required to keep him as virtuous as Rousseau thought he would have to be, if the general will and civic equality were to prevail.

A far less stringent view of citizenship, and one more adapted to the modern state, is the notion of a "citizen-proprietor," as Turgot called him.[15] He came to America in Locke's earlier version. This citizen is normally expected to own external goods, but this is not logically necessary. What he must be able to claim is self-ownership: he must not be a slave. His life and the possessions that sustain it are not secure unless they are legally protected, and to ensure that this is the case the citizen-proprietor must be represented in the lawmaking bodies; otherwise he can be destroyed by taxation or other confiscatory measures. The citizen is an elector and a taxpayer. Access to citizenship might only be open to few men, but such limitations were not inherent in the very idea of the citizen-proprietor, even though originally it did impose limited access to citizenship. Most Americans in the eighteenth century agreed with Blackstone that property qualifications for voting were reasonable in order "to exclude such persons as are of so mean a situation as to be esteemed to have no will of their own."[16] The Declaration of Independence, however, speaks only of the rights to "life, liberty and the pursuit of happiness" of all men and of the consent of the governed, and it was to be the rock upon which all American opponents of exclusion from citizenship would stand. The moral stability gained from property was their opponents' strongest case. Both sides, however, accepted the importance of individual "independence" for citizenship in a representative republic.

Ruling, military valor, subjection by birth or consent, legislating directly or through representatives, property-owning: these are merely the most celebrated qualifications for citizenship in the various regimes, and not the sum of those known to students of political theory. I have mentioned them partly as a background to American thinking about citizenship, but especially to bring out just how distinctive it has been. No historically significant form of government or of citizenship is in principle incompatible with the exclusion of large groups of people, but natural-rights theory makes it very difficult to find good reasons for excluding anyone from full political membership in a modern republic. To be sure, Americans have always found plenty of ideological reasons, from racism to social Darwinism, from religious bigotry to nativism, to justify exclusionary and discriminatory policies. Racism and sexism generally did most of this work of repudiation, and they did it very successfully for a very long time. Nor did they ever disappear. When eventually they did give way to political reality, the barriers to citizenship, piece by piece, had to come down. I do not mean to suggest that this was either quick or easy or even inevitable, but only that after long and painful struggles the inherent political logic of American representative democracy, based on political equality, did prevail.

Indeed from the first, prevalent beliefs made the struggle for the vote extremely intense. The whole rhetoric of the Revolution proclaimed the sole legitimacy of government based on elections by numerical majorities of "We the People," and the rejection of every other form of representation. Those who demanded the vote were not up against aristocratic or monarchical principles of government, but against a representative democracy that falsely ascribed personal deficiencies to them, in order to treat them as lesser beings than "We the People." The excluded were not merely deprived of casual political privileges, they were being betrayed and humiliated by their fellow-citizens.

That is not all. The easy acceptance early on of voting as an expression of personal interests and preferences made citizenship independent of displays of

virtue. No one had to be heroic to vote. It was more an
act of self-promotion than of self-sacrifice, as Hamilton certainly recognized in his famous account of how
elections worked and were expected to function in a
free society.[17] To rule, to fight, and to make laws are
all civic activities, and so is voting to protect one's
interests, but it alone can simply be performed by one
and all. For all of us have interests, and there is no
obvious reason to exclude anyone from citizenship,
since citizens are not expected to demonstrate virtue to
qualify. Bodin's and Hobbes's citizen-subject, to be
sure, need not be particularly patriotic either, but he
simply does nothing at all except obey. He finds his
place in civil society rather than in the public sphere,
but he is no slave, as Hobbes was quick to note.[18]
When, however, every living person is said to have
rights to protect and interests to promote as a citizen,
then exclusion from public life is a denial of his civic
personality and social dignity, as well as a crude indifference to his interests. Indeed, the American Revolution was fought largely as a protest against such political conditions.

It has often been remarked that in the years before
the Revolution, Americans were very quick to complain that if the British government did not meet their
demands, they were little better than slaves. This rhetoric was in part borrowed from English sources, but
as many a contemporary noted, the meaning of the
word *slave* in America was not a mere metaphor for
reduced political independence. It meant something

far more concrete: the actual condition of most American blacks. And that this was a nightmare, though not a probability, for whites in America was at least in part due to the condition of indentured servants, who though far better off than black slaves were close enough to them to engrave the terror of enslavement upon many minds.[19] Dr. Johnson might well heap scorn upon the liberal ideology and pretensions of slave-holders, but as Edmund Burke observed, the two were intimately related.

In his famous speech on the American conflict, Burke turned to the peculiarities of the local culture. "[In] Virginia and the Carolinas," he observed, "they have a multitude of slaves. Where this is the case in any part of the world, those who are free are by far the most proud and jealous of their freedom. Freedom is to them not only an enjoyment, but a kind of rank and privilege . . . In such a people, the haughtiness of dominion combines with the spirit of freedom, fortifies it and renders it invincible."[20] Or as a modern historian, Edmund Morgan, has lately put it, "Virginians may have had a special appreciation of the freedom dear to republicans, because they saw every day what life was like without it."[21] And so Americans saw slavery everywhere, especially in any diminution of what they regarded as their rights.

To be sure, the Southern mixture of extremes makes perfectly good psychological sense. But morally and politically it is incoherent, and was seen as such by New England pamphleteers, especially by the most famous one, James Otis. "[The colonists] would be men, citizens and British subjects after all. No act of parliament . . . can make slaves, not only of one, but of two millions of the commonwealth. [The] colonists, black and white born here, are free born British subjects, and entitled to all the civil rights of such."[22] Here the logic of freedom is uniquely grasped. Perhaps it was because of his intellectual isolation that Otis was to end his life in a lunatic asylum. He certainly adopted the common republican rhetoric of slavery or freedom, but by invoking black men and their fate, he made it evident that he, at least, knew exactly what slavery meant. It is obvious that most Americans were engaging "in hyperbole of truly appalling dimensions" when they compared their position under English rule to the condition of their own black slaves.[23] Of Otis it must, however, be said that he at any rate escaped from the prevailing hypocrisy and moral blindness by being an outspoken and militant abolitionist who insisted that freedom had to be indivisible and universal to be worthy of the name.[24] In this he was unique.

Precisely because Otis did not use the word *slavery* loosely, but in its exact meaning, his identification of his own situation as such does seem like a particularly wild exaggeration. He was, after all, in not the slightest danger of being bought or sold. Nevertheless, because he was not just complaining about having less political power and influence than other Englishmen but also about a loss of social standing, of being degraded, his use of the word *slave* made good rhetorical sense to men who did not share his honest realism about slavery, but who certainly could grasp the force of his metaphors. For there are two quite distinct elements in Otis's assault on Parliament. He wanted American Englishmen to be represented in Parliament on the same "virtual" terms as European ones, because otherwise their interests were not properly protected and they could be taxed and regulated in unacceptable ways. This is representation, that is, full citizenship in the British Empire, as a means to an end, to the pursuit of one's interests and as a form of ongoing political activity. The second element was that having a voice in Parliament was a matter of prestige, of public recognition.

Otis did not call for equal representation, or for a wider suffrage; he seemed to be content with the prevailing English system of highly unequal representation. He did, however, feel demeaned by being excluded altogether, as an American, in a way that men just like him in England were not. These men had representatives for whom they might not have been able to vote personally, but who were elected by members of their class and general locality. Moreover, eventually they might become electors. As an American he was permanently voiceless, and so counted for less than other Englishmen.

The Revolutionary generation was soon to reject virtual representation in favor of the local far more popular electoral system, and when they did so, the same two notes were sounded. The Colonists were to be heard and served. If Colonists must obey Parliament, then they must make sure that its laws were made in their interests and by men who understood and were well informed about them. "With regards to parliament, 'tis possible they may have been misinformed and deceived." With local representation, "both countries [would have] a thorough knowledge of each other's interests."[25] And in this context, knowledge meant an appreciative and detailed understanding of colonial interests as well as of the colonists' political standing.

Though there were property qualifications for voting, representation was actual and not virtual in the American Colonies. Most white men had the vote, and to be represented meant to be spoken for, but it was also a matter of being there, being heard, counting, having a sense of "somebodyness" as a black voter was to say many years later.[26] Certainly virtual representation by Europeans could not accomplish that for Americans. Englishmen were too remote from them culturally and politically to understand them fully or to speak for them. In any case, by then they had rejected the old system in the name of the rights of man. They wanted not merely to be represented, but to be electors.

In retrospect it seems clear that universal white manhood suffrage had been implicitly promised to all American citizens by their leaders from the onset of the conflict with Great Britain, yet it took over half a century to fulfill it, because equality of rights had from the first had its enemies. In the debates about universal suffrage no name was invoked more often than Jefferson's, and not surprisingly, since the Declaration of Independence was the best possible argument for democratic reform. It was, indeed, in the course of that second, democratizing era of American politics, the so-called age of Jackson, that Jefferson became the "Saint of Monticello." In fact, however, the ideas presented at the state constitutional conventions which were called to deal with demands for political democratization were far older than the American republic. Like so much else in American political thought, these ideas had their origins in Puritan England, and especially in the Putney Debates of 1647 in which Cromwell and his son-in-law, Henry Ireton, were confronted by the radical officers of their army.[27]

"We judge," one of the officers said, "that all inhabitants that have not lost their birthright should have an equal voice in elections." Moreover, they "[did] think that the poorest man in England is not at all bound in a strict sense to that government that he has not had a voice to put himself under." They "would fain know what we have fought for" since the laws that enslave the people of England were still in force and "that they should be bound by the laws in which they have no voice at all." They felt not just excluded, but betrayed. "I wonder," one officer cried out, "we were so much deceived. If we had not a right to the kingdom, we were mere mercenary soldiers." They had certainly believed in the promise of a new order: "All here, both great and small, think we fought for something."

Against these claims of the citizen's "birthright," Ireton pitted a powerful argument for the primacy of property rights and a franchise limited to men who had freeholds. They alone had "a permanent, fixed interest in this kingdom." Moreover, if you "admit any man that has a breath and being . . . this will destroy property." How, indeed, could one have any law at all, if it could be challenged in the name of just anyone's birthright? Landed property, especially, is fundamental. The men who owned the land owned England, and they certainly did have a stake in it. Ireton's case was surely not trivial, but neither was the cry of the soldiers, especially against the insult of being mere hired mercenaries rather than citizen-soldiers who had fought for a just cause.

Quite apart from their intrinsic dramatic interest, these debates have a permanent significance, especially for American political thought. Not only did the soldiers claim that voting was a birthright, they proclaimed voting to be the most basic and characteristic political act of the citizen-soldier. Citizenship and voting had become inseparable. The future American citizen was born in the course of these exchanges. Nor is that all. The opponents of these views were to be just as important in the United States. All their arguments were repeated over and over again whenever yet another group of Americans demanded the right to vote.

It is as if Ireton had given a permanent structure to the arguments of all opponents of universal suffrage, and to all who saw it as a threat to property, and who feared men who had no stake in their country.

After the Civil War race and gender replaced property as the disqualifications that left white males, and them alone, in a position to vote in elections. Like their enfranchised predecessors, they too now did not want to admit others to citizenship. The fear of being robbed and displaced by the social outsider came to haunt them too. It was an anxiety that was as impervious to solid, empirically grounded arguments as it was to moral reproof. It nourished itself. Not until very recently, when the last barriers to universal adult suffrage were removed, did this entire edifice of argument fall into disuse, to be all but forgotten.

One of the reasons why the ideology of the rebellious soldiers of Cromwell's army appealed so readily to Americans was that their situation was not at all dissimilar. Only Vermont had manhood suffrage in 1780, when many a veteran announced in vain that "we have fought for the right of voting and we will now exercise it."[28] Jacksonian radicalism received a powerful stimulus from the veterans of the War of 1812. The agitation for the abolition of property qualifications for voting and for equal representation according to population began shortly after the war ended, though it was completed only several decades later, after state constitutional conventions finally could no longer stall in the face of overwhelmingly popular clamor for reform.

The popularity of democratic reform, the fact that the new Western states all had universal manhood suffrage with no ill effects, and the Jeffersonian legacy all constituted a vast difference between Jacksonian America and post-Napoleonic Europe and even England as it lurched toward the Reform Act. But the greatest difference of all between the two continents was American slavery. The very vocabulary of politics was molded by it, and distinguished it from European arguments. English radicals for centuries grumbled on occasion about being "enslaved," but their real problem was class, not race and slavery. Their cry was Colonel Rainborough's immortal "the poorest he that is in England has a life to live as the greatest he."[29] But in every American state slavery, not mere poverty, hung like a cloud over every debate, even in states in which the peculiar institution did not exist. Thus in Massachusetts speakers on behalf of abolishing property qualifications for voting began by noting that the consequences of having the vote were insignificant, but that it was "ardently desired" because without the vote, "men who have no property are put in the situation of the slaves of Virginia; they ought to be saved from the degrading feeling."[30] It was a powerful argument.

To appreciate fully the degree to which slavery dominated these debates, however, one must turn to the Virginia Convention of 1829–1830. Like their English forebears, the reformers spoke eloquently of their military services to their country. "If landless citizens have been ignominiously driven from the polls, in time of peace, they have at least been generously summoned, in war, to the battlefield. Nor have they disobeyed the summons, or, less profusely than others, poured out their blood in defense of their country."[31] Even this citizen-soldier plea, however, was conditioned by slavery. As another reformer reminded his fellow-Virginians, "The slave-holding states are fast approaching a crisis . . . a time when every freeman will be needed—when every man must be at his post . . . Let us give no reason for any to stand back, or refuse their service in the cause of their country."[32] Good arms and good laws were urgently called for in defense of slavery some thirty years before the outbreak of the Civil War.

The most frequent and heartfelt cry of the disenfranchised Westerners in Virginia was, however, that without the vote they were slaves. The minority of Easterners, who owned slaves, would grow ever smaller, and the weaker they became, the more despotic would be their rule over the Western majority, who owned few slaves. They "look to our perpetual slavery," the Westerners complained. Eventually out-of-state buyers of a slave plantation would face the following prospect: they would behold "a hundred wretches exposed to sale, singly or in families, with their master's land," and if they bought it all, "they would instantly become Sovereigns in this free land, and the present possessor would become their slave . . . Your doctrine makes me a slave. So long as you hold political dominion over me, I am a slave." This man clearly knew exactly what slavery was. It was no metaphor for him; it was the ultimate threat to his standing, and he feared it.[33] A New Yorker might buy him!

The vote was so important to these men because it meant that they were citizens, unlike women and slaves, as they repeated over and over again. Their very identity as free males was at stake. Their opponents had taunted them with the reminder that if the vote was a natural right, then women and blacks should vote. The former were as good if not better than men, and the latter, though certainly inferior, were men by nature. Together these people constituted a majority of the population, moreover. These were certainly very threatening arguments for white males, and the answers were just what one might expect, that nature had made women so weak as to require male protection, and blacks so stunted that slavery was their true condition. The civil standing that these creatures could *not* have, defined its importance for the white male, because it distinguished him from the majority of his degraded inferiors.

With this in mind, being a voter became the ambition of all disenfranchised Virginians and made some of them eloquent. The right of suffrage, they argued, should not be understood in "its technical and confined sense, the right to vote for public functionaries only . . . in an enlarged sense it is the right by which a man signifies his will to become a member of Government, of the social compact." In short, it is what makes him a citizen. "Suffrage," this speaker went on to say, "is the substratum, the paramount right" upon which all the others, to life, liberty, property, and the pursuit of happiness, rest.[34]

The opponents of universal manhood suffrage did nothing to diminish its social importance. On the contrary, they thought it too valuable to be shared with men who had no property and no stake in their country. No one expressed his fears better than Chancellor Kent of New York: "The tendency of universal suffrage is to jeopardize the rights of property and the principles of liberty . . . there is a tendency in the poor to covet and to share the plunder of the rich . . . there is a tendency in ambitious and wicked men to inflame these combustible materials. The notion that every man that works a day on the road, or serves an idle hour in the militia is entitled as of right to an equal participation in the whole power of government . . . has no foundation in justice . . . Society is an association for the protection of property as well as of life, and the individual who contributes only one cent to the common stock, ought not to have the same power and influence . . . as he who contributes a thousand."[35]

There are several arguments involved in the conservative case. In their view, voting was not one of the privileges and immunities of American citizenship; it was a special grant to be conferred by state law as a matter of public policy. Moreover, it was to be given only to property owners, who automatically gained prudence and probity through possessions. Finally, they did not see America as an association of citizens, but as a joint-stock company in which each partner received benefits in proportion to his investments.

It did not turn out to be very difficult to rebut these fears. There had been no threats to property in the states that already had universal manhood suffrage. Virtue did not, moreover, come with property; on the contrary, wealth corrupted men, according to the traditional republican ideology. If one wanted to create upright citizens, one ought to support public education, real schooling for citizenship, rather than reducing the poor to semi-slavery. The republic was an association of persons united by a contract, not a business corporation, and citizens had an equal claim to their rights.

These arguments prevailed, within limits. For while the victorious democrats rejected wealth as a sign of virtue, they instantly replaced it with race. The citizen-soldiers of New York complained that blacks did not serve in the militia and were unfit to vote as a result. They were reminded that this was not the fault of blacks, but of the militia, but this proved unavailing. The radicals who had just voted for universal male suffrage instantly did their best to disenfranchise most of the free blacks of the state, who had the right to vote. Their argument was simple racism. It imputed a lack of virtue to all blacks as such, though the worst white scoundrel was declared fit to vote, as the conservative opponents of this measure noted. The year was 1821, and it established the unyielding political habits of democratic racism, which are still with us.

However, while many a Jacksonian democrat was untrue to his professed egalitarian principles, his arguments served black Americans well after the Civil War, when America was transformed. Perhaps even more than their predecessors, the freedmen saw the vote as a mark of social standing. It was, after all, *the* public sign that their years of servitude were over, and that they were citizens at last. It is extraordinary, in fact, how very mainstream American the ideology and aspirations of the ex-slaves were. What they wanted was to be citizens like everyone else, and that meant voting.

We need only listen to Frederick Douglass to grasp the intensity of black feeling on the subject: "Slavery is not abolished until the black man has the ballot."[36] The black man could, moreover, now claim to be a genuine citizen-soldier after his services in the Civil War. "It is dangerous to deny any class of people the right to vote. But the black man deserves the right to vote for what he has done, to aid in suppressing the rebellion, both by fighting and by assisting the Federal soldier wherever he was found. He deserves to vote because his services may be needed again," noted Douglass.[37] "If he knows enough to shoulder a musket and to fight for the flag, fight for the government, he knows enough to vote." And finally, "Shall we be citizens in war, and aliens in peace?"[38] Nothing could come closer to the cry "Are we mercenaries?" hurled at Ireton in the Putney Debates. Here as there the citizen-soldier was democratized. He was no longer a virtuous martial hero but a voter, a bearer of rights, and not of a remarkable social character. Nor was Douglass alone. "The logical result of military service," a Republican senator insisted, "was that the black man is henceforth to assume a new status among us."[39]

For Northern Republicans it seemed to be a matter of simple equity. It was their duty "to see that no man who had voted for the flag should be under the feet of him who had insulted it," according to one senator. To be sure, party interest was also involved in Republican support of the Fifteenth Amendment, since they expected to get the black vote in the North.[40]

In spite of these expectations the black citizen-soldiers did not really achieve parity of status, and in the Second World War they again had to remind white Americans that they had heeded Douglass's call, "Men of color—to arms!" They had fought for the four freedoms and against fascism abroad, and now these veterans returned to claim as much at home.[41] It is a tribute to their faith in the ideal of the citizen-soldier that after so many years of disappointment they should have once again raised this claim. It was a demand for their rightful public standing in a republic, and not just a debt that was owed them for their services in a terrible war.

Standing was not all that Douglass and the Republican Radicals expected from the ballot. Douglass rejected educational qualifications for the freedmen or any other citizens, because the vote would have in itself a moral impact upon the newly enfranchised voter; it was a path to his maturity. "Education is great but manhood is greater. The one is the principle, the other the accident. Man was not made as an attribute to education, but education as an attribute to man . . . Take the ballot from the Negro and you take from him the means and motive that make for an education."[42] And in his famous essay "What the Black Man Wants," he summed up the whole case for black suffrage and its primary importance to the freedmen as an instrument of social advancement: "Without [enfranchisement], his liberty is a mockery; without this you might as well almost retain the old name of slavery for his condition; for in fact, if he is not the slave of the individual master, he is the slave of society and holds his liberty as a privilege, not as a right. He is at the mercy of the mob, and has no means of protecting himself."[43]

In this passage Douglass is thinking of the vote as a means of self-protection, as a form of political agency, which would empower the black man and allow him to promote his interests. "The ballot was a tool; upon its use would depend its real value," on this common view.[44] Even the veteran abolitionist Wendell Phillips thought that "a man with a ballot in his hand is the master of the situation . . . The ballot is opportunity, education, fair play, right to office, and elbow room." The black population could now take care of its own interests.[45]

Voting as effective political action proved less than practical. It was, in fact, a thoroughly dangerous assumption. Abolitionists like Senator Richard Yates believed quite genuinely that "the ballot will finish the negro question; it will settle everything . . . the ballot is the freedman's Moses."[46] What the winning of the vote permitted him and many other war-weary abolitionists to do was to forget about the black man, since he was now all set to take care of himself by himself, with the ballot in hand. Black enfranchisement may indeed have touched every portion of the Southern social fabric, but not for long. The vote could not protect the black Southerner against grotesque registration requirements, literacy tests, poll taxes, grandfather clauses, white primaries, and more chicanery than they could possibly defeat.

When these impediments to voting and representation were finally lifted, by the Voting Rights Act of 1965 and one by one by court decisions, discussion was limited to the implementation of recognized rights, to overcoming obstruction. Even the old notion that the vote was fundamental as "the right preservative of other basic civil and political rights" had its recognized ambiguities. In actuality the right is not fundamental because it secures benefits or other rights directly for the individual voter acting alone; it does so only if he or she votes as a member of a group. For even though public services certainly improved for blacks as soon as they were free to vote, these were collective, not personal, gains. To promise more is to ensure the disappointment of the newly enfranchised voters and to make voting appear a more futile and frustrating gesture than it in fact is. The social circumstances and daily lives of new voters will not be quickly altered by voting. Voting is the necessary first step, but in itself it is not enough; additional forms of social and political action are required to promote and protect the interests and rights of ordinary citizens.[47] The deepest impulse for demanding the suffrage arises from the recognition that it is the characteristic, the identifying, feature of democratic citizenship in America, not a means to other ends. It is enough to say with W. E. B. Du Bois that "voting is necessary to modern manhood."[48] To promise more is bound to lead to disillusionment; to say less is needlessly cynical.

"We want [the vote]," Douglass wrote, "because it is our *right,* first of all. No class of men can, without insulting their own nature, be content with any deprivation of their rights. We want it again, as a means for educating our race. Men are so constituted that they derive their conviction of their own possibilities largely from the estimate formed of them by others. If nothing is expected of a people, that people will find it difficult to contradict that expectation. By depriving us of suffrage, you affirm our incapacity to form intelligent judgments respecting public measures." In a monarchy it would not matter if he, along with everyone else, did not have the vote, but where government is based on the idea of universal suffrage "to rule us out is to make us an exception, to brand us with the stigma of inferiority."[49] No clearer statement of the idea of citizenship as standing could be imagined. This is hardly surprising, since the fear of slavery had always been at the very core of this particular conception of citizenship. Who should express it better than an American ex-slave?

If the Fifteenth Amendment did not do nearly enough for the black voter, it did nothing at all for women. And the result was bitter resentment. The women's suffrage movement had grown directly out of abolitionism, but when disenfranchised women saw black men achieve a right that they still lacked, their deep racism quickly asserted itself, and it grew worse as they began to seek the support of Southern women. This unhappy chapter in the women's suffrage movement is particularly relevant to my story, because it illuminates the darker side of citizenship as standing. Women had every reason to feel betrayed and their anger was hardly unjustified, but they shared the prejudices of their class and time and judged their own worth in terms of prevailing standards. By those measures they were better than many men who had the vote, and their disenfranchisement was an affront to their social standing.

There is nothing equal about social standing in general. Nothing is more unequally distributed than social respect and prestige. It is only citizenship perceived as a natural right that bears a promise of equal political standing in a democracy. It is, however, always possible to make a claim for the vote on grounds of superior, not equal, standing, as the advocates of property qualifications had done in the past. Women demanding the suffrage found that their cause might be better served by treating voting as a privilege limited to the educated and respectable, such as their own middle-class selves. It was in vain that Douglass, their supporter, pointed out the greater needs of the freedmen, compared to the many advantages enjoyed by these women. They did not see the difference between someone who can exercise all the privileges of legal citizenship except the vote, and someone who had no rights that a white man need respect, in the celebrated phrase of the *Dred Scott* decision.

When Wendell Phillips said, "One question at a time. This hour belongs to the Negro," the suffragettes walked out on him.[50] They saw their standing as above the black man's, and they acted accordingly. It was a short-sighted move. Having themselves so often spoken of voting as a privilege, when they compared themselves to freedmen and new immigrants, they need hardly have been surprised when in 1875 the courts told them that it was not a right and that they could do without it, since they already possessed all civil rights.[51]

Standing was as much an issue for the women's suffrage movement as it had been for its predecessors in the history of the battle for the vote, but there were many quite novel features to this last of the campaigns for legal enfranchisement. For one thing, after the

Emancipation Proclamation slavery was at last reduced to a figure of speech. Political inequality, however, did survive, and it was particularly galling for
women in a country where every male now had the
vote, and where to be without it put one below the
human norm. They were certainly not slaves, but they
were politically degraded. As Elizabeth Cady Stanton
put it, "To deny political equality is to rob the os-
tracized of self-respect; of credit in the market place; of
recompence in the world; of voice in [the choice] of
those who make and administer the law; a choice in
the jury before which they are tried, and in the judge
who decides their punishment."[52] Not to be heard is
not to exist, to have no visibility and no place politically.

There were, however, some arguments that women
could not really make. They were not and did not
want to be soldier-citizens, as they now can be. Instead
they did emphasize their contribution to the war effort
of the North,[53] but it was not a wholly satisfactory
substitute. As for the ancient claim that they were the
mothers of republican heroes, it had only confined
women to the home in both theory and practice.[54] It
was not a serviceable proposition for radical women
and was not revived. Indeed, virtue arguments, long
the staple of conservatives, were especially problem-
atic for women. If they were superior without the
vote, why give it to them? Nevertheless, women did
use virtue arguments of one kind. Both Stanton and

Susan Anthony argued that since Africans, Irish, and other inferior alien males had the vote, why not "women of wealth, education, virtue and refinement?"[55]

Natural rights and the Declaration of Independence continued to be invoked by women, but the second half of the nineteenth century was generally not hospitable to these remnants of the Enlightenment. Social Darwinism, health and hygiene-oriented reform, and the Social Gospel were notably undemocratic paths to progress, and the women's movement became a part of this intellectual mainstream. Liberalism had also altered, moving from civic freedom to a concern for self-development and the nurture of the individual personality. For women interested in the suffrage, voting increasingly was just one step toward the fulfillment of these immensely personal ends. If the cry "no taxation without representation" still meant much to the more radical and economically astute feminists, it had come to mean less than the more personal demand to be recognized as a unique individual who could express herself significantly in private and in public. To be sure, this ideology also reflected the domestic situation of these women, and the stifling myths that encased it. The real irony was that because women had adopted the dominant attitudes of their time and place so completely, their final victory led to no noticeable political change at all. When women finally went to the polls, it turned out to be the biggest non-event in our electoral history. Women wanted their standing as citizens, but they were neither an ascriptive social group nor a distinct political class. They were just like the men of their families—good enough citizens, no more and no less.

Unlike blacks, women were never again deprived of the vote, but it did not alter their social lives significantly. Those members of the suffrage movement who had seen it as an instrument of social transformation were wholly unrealistic. Nor did the vote raise the social opportunities of women. What it achieved was to remove a stigma that weighed particularly heavily upon them. And it did so because of the promise of democracy and because of the knowledge that they had, in one respect at least, shared the degrading lot of the slaves, whose half-enfranchised descendants were not entirely invisible or forgettable. Above all, the rejection of hereditary distinctions, the very core of the American political credo, made disenfranchisement on grounds of color and sex intolerable. From the first it was universally accepted that America would have no titles of nobility and no inherited political privileges. Race and slavery are, however, hereditary conditions, and one is born a woman. These are all birthmarks, and they could not forever limit the birthright of American citizens.

In spite of all the obstacles thrown in its way by injustice and discrimination in all its many forms, the vote was won, but not that other emblem of equal citizenship, the opportunity to earn one's livelihood. The Great Society was a triumph for voting, but its struggle against poverty and unemployment was not a success. All adult Americans are now constituents, equal voters in their districts, but they are not equally independent, and too many do not earn anything.

CHAPTER TWO

EARNING

MODERN citizenship is not confined to political activities and concerns. Important as governing, voting, military service, and taxpaying are, they are not nearly as significant as the endeavors that constitute what Hegel called "civil society."[1] It is in the marketplace, in production and commerce, in the world of work in all its forms, and in voluntary associations that the American citizen finds his social place, his standing, the approbation of his fellows, and possibly some of his self-respect.[2] The spheres designated as public and as private, respectively, are always shifting, and civil society, which combines both, has no set contours. In America it has generally been treated as the sphere of private choices, but the legal structure, meaning, and character of these transactions are public, and they affect the whole republic. Economic exchanges and entitlements are ultimately subject to public sanction, and so are the activities of the many voluntary organizations that have always been a feature of American public life. Earning and spending are hardly private in the sense that prayer or love might be.

The individual American citizen is in fact a member of two interlocking public orders, one egalitarian, the other entirely unequal. To be a recognized and active citizen at all he must be an equal member of the polity, a voter, but he must also be independent, which has all along meant that he must be an "earner," a free remunerated worker, one who is rewarded for the actual work he has done, neither more nor less. He cannot be a slave or an aristocrat.

Aristocrats and slaves are both anomalies in a republic of equal citizens. The first are proscribed in name by the Constitution, which prohibits titles of nobility and all that they imply. However, aristocratic aspirations and assertions did not entirely disappear in actuality from civil society; many rich Americans continued to yearn for European distinctions. But these affectations were not remotely as significant as slavery, which was a public and private curse that distorted the politics of a modern republic from the first. Its evil consequences still mar it, long after its legal repudiation. It was in the context of these two incongruities that the model of the independent citizen-earner developed, and it was against them that those who aspired to realize it had to assert their standing. The American work ethic, which seems so odd to many social observers now, becomes perfectly comprehensible when it is understood not as a reflection of the class values of pre-industrial artisans, but as the ideology of citizens caught between racist slavery and aristocratic pretensions. It has endured because the political conditions to which it responded from the first have not disappeared. No less enduring has been the dream of self-employment, which is the very epitome of social independence.

The men who forged the work ethic in Jacksonian America did not shun these facts; on the contrary, they were deeply aware of them and of the novelty of their society. They were consciously new men, born within a new and imperfect republic, and they said so. Their understanding of their situation, between the equally unacceptable conditions of idle elites and unpaid slaves, was accurate. It has survived because it remains plausible. This also suggests that there may be an implicit right to work embedded in this enduring ideology.

From the first, the new American citizen was a modern, not a classical, republican. Traditionally it had been thought that republics needed virtuous, wholly public citizens in order to remain free. When the modern extended, representative republic was created in 1787, it was not based on virtue, however, but on independent agents and the free play of their interests. In this respect they would follow the pattern of unfettered religious sectarianism to the general benefit of all. The most celebrated defense of this view of citizenship was Madison's contribution to the *Federalist Papers,* but soon there were many more, and it became the dominant view, as anti-federalist anxieties were duly calmed. A representative democracy, it was agreed, depends on the fluid interaction of multiple interests to function freely, and these interests were generally sectional and economic. To have an interest and protected rights to pursue it cannot by any stretch of the imagination be called virtue, but it does imply that their bearers have a recognized public standing. Such citizenship requires that they be independent persons in both their political and civil roles, who give and withdraw their votes from their representatives and political parties as they see fit, and who sell their labor, but not themselves. No slave can have an interest, because he has no public or civil standing. Nor can the claims of a political monopolist be accepted, because he actively threatens the entire political order of freely competing interests.

Persons and groups that pursue interests and ideologies that are designed to destroy such a republic cannot be recognized, though they cannot usually be proscribed. From the first, Americans feared conspiratorial aristocratic and monarchical cabals. And to these, fear of Jacobins and other European revolutionary ideologies were soon added. In the Jacksonian period apprehension of a new aristocracy of monopolists, and especially the men who ran the Bank of the United States, flared up with exceptional vigor. The campaign against the Bank and the long struggle for universal white manhood suffrage aroused enormous resentments, but they also forged an ideology of work that has never lost its preeminence.

In the wake of the Jacksonian assertion of democratic beliefs America was left, not an egalitarian, but a republican ethos, which saw the independence of the working and earning many constantly threatened by the idle, aristocratic few at one end of the spectrum, and by slavery at the other. Both were anomalies in a republic that was based on the premise that independent citizens acted in a republic economy in which each had an equal opportunity to get ahead by his own efforts and could earn his bread without fear or favor. This vision of economic independence, of self-directed "earning," as the ethical basis of democratic citizenship took the place of an outmoded notion of public virtue, and it has retained its powerful appeal. We are citizens only if we "earn."

The most general nineteenth-century ideology that originally sustained this public view of earning in America has been aptly called "parallelism."[3] The individual citizen may expect to improve his social position by hard work because he lives in a democratic and constantly progressing society, and uninterrupted social progress is in turn assured because Americans are hard-working and public-spirited democrats. They create the public wealth which each one of them may hope to share. No one doubted the labor theory of value which declared that labor had created all wealth, and each citizen expected to benefit from the products of his work. If a citizen was to gain he had to produce, and the more the better, both for himself and his family and for the republic as a whole.

The addiction to work that this induced was noted by every visitor to the United States in the first half of the nineteenth century. So was the passion for money, which, as the most astute noted, meant not just gain but also independence, the freedom to do with one's life as one pleased. To have money is to spend and save and give as one chooses, without asking leave of any superior. It had taken the place that honor occupied in aristocratic societies.[4] "Equality makes not only work itself, but work specifically to gain money, honorable," Tocqueville noted.[5] And indeed, independence had replaced honor as the object of social aspiration. It was an enormously radical change. Independent citizens in a democratic order had now not only to be respected for working, they also had a right to self-improvement, to education and unblocked opportunities for self-advancement. These rights were partly a fulfillment of the promise of equality enshrined in the Declaration of Independence, and partly they were the necessary corollary of the duty to contribute to the progress and prosperity of the republic. For the individual citizen, this also meant that socially he was what he did as an earner at any given moment in his life. One is what one does in such a world.

The sheer novelty of the notion of the dignity of labor in general, and as an essential element of citizenship, can scarcely be exaggerated. It was one of the many contributions of the Enlightenment to American public culture that flourished here far more than it ever could in Europe.[6] In the past it had been almost universally believed that physical work defiles us, that those who labor are impure. Certainly the philosophers of antiquity regarded productive and commercial work as so deeply degrading that it made a man unfit for citizenship. Nor did these attitudes disappear with slavery. European society was for centuries separated into three orders: those who pray, those who fight, and those who labor. The last were the despised peasantry, hardly to be distinguished from the beasts. Nor is biblical religiosity reassuring. We must work as a punishment for sin, and the Pauline injunction to work hard at one's calling does nothing to diminish the sense of pain, confinement, and oppression implied in the obligation to bear the yoke of industry.

Of all these inducements to look at labor as a disgrace and a curse, none has lasted longer than aristocratic and intellectual disdain. The atavistic contempt for physical work has never died out. To be "in trade" was a real social stigma throughout the last century and is hardly admired even now in England. One need only recall that Grace Kelly's father could not row at Henley because he had worked with his hands as a young man. Nor were these attitudes unknown in America, as many an amazed visitor was to note. There has certainly always been enough quasi-aristocratic pride in America to dismay democrats. And there is a degree of silliness in the fact that the Sons and Daughters of the American Revolution should be such colossal snobs.

Admiration for inherited family "names," rooted in the most primitive beliefs about the transmission of "noble blood," has been no less enduring than the contempt for work. Only the divine right of kings and their vicarious political authority did not outlast the eighteenth century. In political philosophy, however, utility had for some time been the real ground of governmental legitimacy. The social policies of mercantilist states, whether Protestant or Catholic, keenly encouraged industriousness and work, but that did not necessarily impinge upon their political values. In England, to be sure, economists excoriated not only the idle poor but also the idle rich as a "general leprosy," particularly when compared to the hard-working Dutch.[7]

And in John Locke's writings we can see an even more fateful novelty. In his plan for the education of a young gentleman, a boy who was expected to grow up to become a member of a governing class, manual work and accounting play an important part. They are useful, Locke noted, and it is rational and becoming to be useful.[8] Moreover, while government derives its just powers from the consent of the governed in Locke's view, the purpose of government is to make itself useful to them. That is why they decided to form a political order in the first place. The implications of these propositions were fully accepted only in America, and then only gradually. That nothing is more useful than productive work, and that nothing can, therefore, be better, has been so radical an idea and one so much at odds with inherited attitudes that few people have ever really accepted it fully, even those who proclaim it enthusiastically.

In pre-Revolutionary America there were many Puritans to preach the gospel of hard work, but it was

really Benjamin Franklin who divorced the worth of
work from its religious context and gave it a new civic
meaning. He has been much misunderstood, thanks to
Max Weber's misreading. Weber was so obsessed by
the link between Protestantism and the work ethic that
he ignored every other connection, and among these
were democracy and personal independence. Why,
after all, have Chinese, Irish, and Jewish Americans
worked as maniacally as they have? Not because they
were Protestants. Weber could only see a secularized
Puritan capitalist in Franklin, who was "dominated by
the making of money and by acquisition as the ultimate end of life" and "completely devoid of any hedo-
nistic admixture."[9] In fact, Franklin was a bon vivant
and quit business at the age of forty to do other things
with his life. What was unique about his view of work
was that it alone could make one independent, and that
it was a source of pride to be "self-made," that is, the
product of one's own labors.

Consider his last will and testament: "I, Benjamin
Franklin of Philadelphia, printer, late Minister Pleni-
potentiary of the United States of America to the
Court of France, now President of the State of Pennsylvania"[10]—there is enormous pride in these words,
and not only in his achievements, extraordinary
though they were, but also in having done it himself
and by working at trade, the ground of all his later
glory. Even in the trite maxims of Poor Richard we
can find a bold spirit. If you want to be free, "serve
yourself." "Your Creditor has Authority at his Plea-

sure to deprive you of your liberty, by confining you
in Gaol for life, or to sell you for a servant if you
should not be able to pay him . . . The Borrower is a
Slave to the Lender and the Debtor to the Creditor,
disdain the chain, preserve your freedom and maintain
your Independency." If you want to be your own
master, don't be idle. "Be industrious and FREE."[11]

There was, finally, a civic aspect to the idea of work
as well. One worked for oneself and for the community simultaneously. The experiences of daily life
were, moreover, to be put to civic use by the appren-
tices and journeymen whom Franklin organized into a
network of *juntos*. These clubs began by discussing
public events and went on to promote every sort of
civic improvement in Philadelphia: the first lending
library, cleaner and better lighted streets, volunteer
fire-brigades, and more. Rotarianism is the most democratic of nonofficial civic activities, and it was Franklin's invention. But it is the interplay of productive
work, self-improvement, and public concern, the in-
tegration of these lives into a sphere half-private and
half-public, that made these clubs such enduring institutions and also constitutes their peculiar character
and significance. Together with the workplace, they
make up American civil society.

Benjamin Franklin was held up as an example to
every Jacksonian youth, but politically the author of
the Declaration of Independence was their patron saint
in their struggle against the "paper aristocracy." What
did aristocracy mean to radical Jacksonian journalists

and politicians? It meant more than just the possession of wealth. The essence of the democratic definition of aristocracy was, in President Jackson's words, *any* group that by its use of its wealth "exercises more than its just proportion of influence in political affairs." It was not wealth as such that was reprehensibly aristocratic, but wealth either gained through governmental favor or used to buy political power and influence. All monopolists and holders of licenses and charters were aristocrats because they owed their wealth to a governmental grant, and had not earned it by their own efforts. They enjoyed unearned advantages. This was illegitimate or an "artificial inequality of wealth and power," which a democratic government is duty-bound to prevent. However, "equality of talents or of wealth cannot be produced by human institutions," said Jackson.[12] A democratic, egalitarian government of a highly unequal society does not attempt to alter the natural economic order, but it cannot abide legal privileges, smacking ultimately of titles of nobility.

In the Jacksonian view, European feudalism had begun with the distribution of royal grants of land and of political monopolies. "The royal bastard," as Tom Paine called William the Conqueror, had handed over the land to his ruffian band. That may not be what the best medievalists have taught us, but it encapsulated all the fears of these republican citizens. How was any repetition of the European pattern to be avoided? And how were the remnants of this barbarous feudal past to be eliminated? Even Emerson worried that "our government still partakes of that element" of feudalism, because "the public mind lacks self-respect." He certainly did not hesitate to teach his fellow-citizen the worth of self-reliance.[13]

To a true Jacksonian radical it was clear that the best way to prevent the spread of such feudal blemishes was simply to have as little government as possible. The fewer civil service jobs there are, the fewer taxes collected, and the smaller the number of projects undertaken by government, the less harm it can do. And above all, less government means less artificial inequality because the government is deprived of the means to establish an aristocracy of idle drones. The President, however, did have a new and important part to play. He alone represents the people as a whole; all other elected officials speak for only a section or a party of the nation. Only the President can act as the tribune of the people and protect them against the predatory assaults of the money-power and the aristocracy, to whom the laboring classes are always in danger of losing "their fair influence in the government." The independent spirit and the rights of the industrious classes were being sapped by crafty and indolent bankers, and it was the office of the President to protect the rights of democratic citizens against this menace.

The aristocrat is not only a political monopolist, he is a moral and cultural threat to the republic as well. The aristocrat is idle and shows a contempt for work. The merely rich were unobjectionable, but the "*idle* rich" were intolerable. The great division among men in society was not between poor and rich, but between the "do-somethings" and the "do-nothings." Failure to work was not merely immoral in and of itself, it also expressed a social ideology, the contempt for labor. Jacksonian democrats were acutely aware of the traditions that treated work as defiling. That is why so many insisted that by "we the people we mean emphatically the class which labors with its hands."

The democratic party of America, according to William Leggett, was composed of producers, while the aristocrats were consumers, rich and proud. The working classes were the majority, and their "sole reliance" was the equality of rights. That alone stood between them and the aristocracy of "vested interests" and idle wealth.[14] To Stephen Simpson, another Jacksonian journalist and unsuccessful politician, the Declaration of Independence meant that "labor brings neither disqualification nor stigma upon the citizen of the United States in a political capacity." In actuality that promise had not been realized, because as long as there were feudal prejudice and slavery in America, work would be despised and aristocrats would be able to bring both idle manners and monopolistic privileges to a country which had been invented to do away with both. Only education, radically reformed, could eliminate the "prejudice of occupations."[15]

Here the link between work, democracy, and public education was forged into a coherent ideology, with its own history, policy, and sense of the future. It also corresponded to the manners and aspirations of a wide public. A European visitor to the United States wrote that "life in America is delightful in the eyes of him who prefers work to everything else, and with whom work can take the place of everything else . . . the habits of life are those exclusively of working people . . . Woe to whatever is inactive and unproductive. Work and you shall be rich."[16] Everyone was on the make and seemed convinced, in the words of the *Cleveland Leader,* that "one may as well be dead as idle."[17] To be useful was the dominant principle of a nation of laboring republicans, but many democrats were far from sanguine about the loyalty of their wealthy fellow-citizens to this ethos.

Jacksonian democrats took the dignity of work to be a fighting faith because there were Americans around who openly showed their scorn for honest work. Nor were they honest, these "ruffle-shirted counter-hoppers, rolling in wealth acquired by driving shrewd bargains . . . and [becoming] princely exclusives."[18] These idlers clubbed together not only to protect their monopolies but to wall themselves off from the people. They "live without labor," deny that all wealth comes from those who produce, and look upon its creation as disgraceful. American workers, moreover, were beginning to have very good and specific reasons for their worries about the Europeanization of America. The first factory workers in New England might well fear that the aristocrats were turning Lowell into another Manchester.[19]

To avoid the calamity of European degradation, and the specter of artificial inequality generally, there must be not only less government altogether, but also far more *free* education. It was the one public activity that did not worry democrats. Education was looked at entirely as an aspect of citizenship and was designed to democratize the young and to prevent aristocratic tendencies.[20]

Important as education was for democratic status, it was no replacement for personal effort in the race of life. Nothing was more democratic than the ideal of the self-made man—not necessarily the man who builds a fortune by hard work only, but more expansively the model of a perfect human character, of what was called "Young America." This truly new man, whom Emerson idolized, is a youth who has no fixed place in society, nothing inherited, who does not stick to a single role in life and who rejects all efforts to restrict and bind him to a place and status. He is self-reliant because he is socially unfettered, immensely self-created, and the master of many skills. "Who can tell how many Franklins may be among you?" asked the President of the New York Mechanics Society in the 1830s. "Your opportunities are great and liberal. This is a country of self-made men, than which nothing better could be said about any state of society."[21] But it was not nearly open enough for a genuine Jacksonian idealist and a truly democratic radical.

Among other things, workers needed a history of their own if they were to achieve the respectable standing to which sheer labor entitled them. It would begin by recognizing that it is only "the mechanical arts" that have raised man's condition above that of the animals. Not property but "mechanical arts" have civilized us. History is made by the producers, not by the consumers, just as the West was visibly being developed by the industrious many. Certainly there had been progress, especially in the modern world, but it was not due to the famous scientists but to the mechanics. Printing, which is "the preservation of all the arts," was invented by a mechanic. So was the mariners' compass, without which America would not have been found. After that there was the steam engine, again the work of an artificer, and one that has made his life far easier. History books should also stress how many of the distinguished generals and statesmen of the Revolutionary era began life as blacksmiths, bookbinders, and other kinds of manual workers.

The point of such a history was to remind the working youth of America of their real place in their country and in the modern world, and to make all they could of it. Opportunity was the one thing they did not lack, but they did need a better sense of their own worth, and a people's history would certainly encourage them. It is important to note that technology was seen as the creation, the great historical achievement, and the best hope of the workingman in America. It would make life easier for him and everyone else and would also increase the value of his work by improving it. Without nostalgia, the technological age seemed full of possibilities.

Jacksonian democrats were generally opposed to slavery in principle, but not only were they not real abolitionists, they frequently resented anti-slavery agitators, whom they suspected of diverting attention from the indignities suffered by Northern workers. In any case, for all their racism, they could see perfectly clearly that slavery did more than any other institution to bring labor into contempt. The very word *slavery* struck fear into the worker's heart. "Because bondage degrades, cramps, and degenerates man, labor shares in the same disgrace because it is a part of the slave." Where there is slavery, toil is associated with baseness.[22] That the Southern planter was an aristocrat unfit for republican government had long been taken for granted by the opponents of slavery. Among the anti-federalists, Richard Henry Lee had spoken of them as a dissipated and idle aristocracy, Jefferson had bewailed their despotic temper, and every European traveler commented on their feudal airs.[23] Among abolitionists it was commonly understood that the planters were ferocious, improvident, inactive, effeminate, and poorly educated, all thanks to their self-inflicted forced idleness. They too were victims of the slave system.[24]

The specter of slavery could never be entirely dispelled in the North; it was an ever-present anxiety. When the wage system first came under scrutiny, the dependence of the worker was instantly likened to that of a slave. Nor were the defenders of Southern slavery reassuring. George Fitzhugh's *Cannibals All* describes the Southern slave as a capital investment that the owner nourishes carefully. His lot is thus a far happier one than that of the "white slave" of the North, exposed to uncaring poverty as a wage earner. It is hardly surprising, however, that Fitzhugh was not particularly popular in the North. Workers might complain that they were the victims of "wage slavery," but the suggestion that they might be better off as *real* slaves, as a form of capital, did not appeal to them. They were protesting the conditions of labor that they had to endure, not praising slavery. Orestes Brownson was addressing not Northern workers but Southern gentlemen when he praised Southerners for their honesty in calling slaves by their real name and accepting aristocracy as a gift of God.[25]

Even if slavery was limited to black people, the institution as such remained threatening. Racism was scarcely enough to reassure the free worker, and that is why by 1858 many saw that the question of spreading slavery was really this: "Shall labor be degraded?"[26] To make labor honorable was the whole object of the Free Soil and Republican parties from 1850 onward. No one doubted that labor was specifically work to gain money, and it was what made the American an alert and intelligent citizen rather than a dull European proletarian or a slave. To live on the unrewarded labor of others and to make the worker a brute was the curse of Southern culture. It was also known to be an unbearable injustice. Lincoln did not think that a black woman was his equal in all respects, but "in her natural right to eat the bread she earns with her own hands without asking leave of anyone else, she is my equal and the equal of all others."[27]

Lincoln is always a star witness, and he testifies to the fears of early wage earners that they would be degraded to the level of slaves. Speaking first to an agricultural audience and then, less colorfully, to the nation, he forcefully rejected the "mud-sill" theory of labor. To Senator Hammond of South Carolina's claim that "in all social systems there must be a class to do the menial duties, to perform the drudgery of life . . . It constitutes the very mud-sill of society" and that the so-called free wage earners were "essentially slaves," Lincoln replied that a young wage earner was not stuck for life in his position.[28] He was not "forcefully fixed for life" in the condition of a hired hand. To Lincoln, if not to his entire audience, the difference between selling one's labor and selling oneself was clear. The latter was not an unalterable state of affairs. There was, of course, an unquenchable hope here as well, the prospect of self-employment, of being an independent farmer in a still mainly agricultural nation. The existence of cheap land still gave this vision a good deal of plausibility. The shimmering ideal for young America was a "prudent, penniless beginner in the world," who works for wages "awhile" and who, thanks to education and self-discipline, soon becomes his own boss.

Free labor in Lincoln's view still had all its old Jacksonian implications, its hostility to the idle and to the spiritual royalists, as well as its faith in the American political system and in social progress driven by education, work, and technological advances. What Lincoln also makes clear in a few luminous sentences is the intensity of his and his listeners' suspicion that wage labor might amount to wage-slavery and in the end to white slavery itself. If he was able to reject this terror forcefully, however, it was not only because of the obvious fact that the slave was unalterably chained to his rightless place, which the free wage earner was not, but also because he evidently believed that the farm laborer could eventually own his own land. And he believed it without any Jeffersonian trappings about the political superiority of yeomen farmers. He regarded them as no better or worse than anyone else. It was simply assumed that if a white man tried hard enough, he could become an independent citizen-proprietor.[29]

His uneasy audience of farmers and other wage earners may have been less sanguine than Lincoln himself, but there is no denying that his faith has proved very durable, as has his and their basic racism. There was, as we know, no enthusiasm for the Civil War especially among urban Northern workers, and there was plenty of racism. Indeed, if slavery was dreaded as a threat and disliked as an anomaly in a democratic society, the person of the slave was far more deeply detested and despised. Free labor feared slavery, but hated the slave. Yet the general ethos of work was alive among slaves, who also shared Lincoln's social vision. "We understand freedom to mean industry and the enjoyment thereof," a spokesman for the freedmen declared.[30] Indeed, for no group of Americans did the connection between earning and citizenship appear closer. When Frederick Douglass got his first paying job in New Bedford after escaping from the South, he rejoiced, though it was very hard labor. "I was now my own master—a tremendous fact . . . The thought, 'I can work! I can work for a living; I am not afraid of work; I have no Master Hugh to rob me of my earnings'—placed me in a state of independence."

In fact Douglass was a living proof of the tenacity of Jacksonian ideology. "All that any man has a right to expect, ask, give or receive in this world, is fair play. When society has secured this to its members, and the humblest citizen of the republic is put into the undisturbed possession of the natural fruits of his own exertions, there is really very little left for society and government to do." "The spirit of caste" was the black man's greatest enemy. "We are opposed to all aristocracy, whether of wealth, power or learning . . . Equality before the law is to the colored man the crowning point of political wisdom," he wrote in 1871.[31] If the absence of "hereditary distinctions" was the essence of the American political heritage, then racism was bound to disfigure the republic by opening the door to aristocracy.[32] Nor was that all, as Douglass's heir, W. E. B. Du Bois, was to ask: "Can the modern organization of industry, assuming as it does free democratic government and the power of the laboring classes to compel respect for their welfare, — can this system be carried out in the South when half its laboring force is voiceless in the public councils and powerless in its own defence?"[33] If citizenship had from the first demanded free earners, industry now demanded citizens. In truth, the two had always been identical in the aspirations of slaves and radical democrats.

It is hardly surprising that the middle-class feminists who came to resent being excluded from the world of gainful employment should have been quite aware of the intimate bond between earning and citizenship. And the image of the slave was certainly at work in the feminist imagination. John Stuart Mill claimed that after reading *Uncle Tom's Cabin,* he felt that the subjection of married women was worse even than that of an American slave. "I am far from pretending that wives are in general no better treated than slaves; but no slave is a slave to the same lengths, and in so full a sense of the word, as a wife is," he wrote.[34] A close student of American politics, a friend of the abolitionists, and an ardent supporter of women's rights, Mill found the analogy between the oppression of women and chattel slavery simply irresistible. That is also how the revolt against the twin evils of workless masters and forced labor, the original call to abolitionism, came to reverberate among those middle-class women who suffered from unwanted idleness and from dependence on men. They too took up and were sustained by the Jacksonian ideology of work and earned independence.

Labor historians have been at pains to show how remote the independent, self-directing "operative" was from the reality of the wage-earning industrial worker in post–Civil War America with its factories and unemployment. And they have been puzzled by the fact that even when workers came to associate work only with the money they might earn, their old Jacksonian ideology survived unabated.[35] American workers have protested long and vigorously against the appalling demands made upon them by the industrial system, but their struggles are in no way obscured by the recognition that the work ethic survived as a political ideology along with their discontent. If, as I have argued, the source of the ideology of earning is not in the conditions of employment, but in political perceptions, then there is really nothing surprising in its endurance. Resentment of the idle monopolist and aristocrat, and fear of being reduced to the condition of a black slave, or of a black second-class citizen, have not disappeared, because they are grounded in lasting political experiences. The Constitution still prohibits titles of nobility, and idle and snobbish elites are still resented, and the memory of slavery, rendered ever potent by racism, still arouses predictable fears among white workers and haunts blacks. This interpretation of the ethos of earning not only makes sense of its centrality as a social value, it also corresponds to what its proponents have said in the past and continue to say.

Thus the resentment of unproductive aristocrats was as lively in the years following the Civil War as it had been in the age of Jackson. A highly visible plutocracy could be seen with all its idle luxuries, stupendous vulgarity, and upper-class European pretensions in every penny newspaper in *fin de siècle* America, not to mention the writings of Mark Twain. It was in this context that the most trenchant social critic of the time, Thorstein Veblen, came to expose their unwholesome effect upon the productive organization of American society. To the extent that he continued the Jacksonians' assault upon the idle rich he was, in spite of all his iconoclasm, a thoroughly traditional radical, and so were the feminists of his time.

Charlotte Perkins Gilman and Veblen were exact contemporaries, and the gospel of work that they taught was very similar. Both had left the rights-based democratic creed of earlier generations behind them. Their philosophical assumptions were grounded in ideas about social evolution, especially the belief that societies were organic wholes that followed laws of natural development. The whole object of public policy was to keep in step with the demands of this preestablished dynamic order. Since history was a movement toward improvement, any group or institution that was a throwback to an earlier age and that retarded adaptation to the needs of a changing social order was by definition socially evil. Natural rights were no longer intellectually appealing at a time when organic necessity looked like a scientific grounding for progressive ethics to Gilman and many of her contemporaries. That these beliefs could underwrite liberal policies as easily as authoritarian ones became evident only later on.

The case for earning, in Gilman's view, was not that free labor had an intrinsic dignity. The injustice was that a woman's economic status, high or low, had no relation to her work, which was confined to the household. This had not been the case on the farm, where husband and wife were real working partners, but it had become the condition of middle-class women, who were essentially idle slaves. Their situation was degrading for them and was also a dysfunctional refusal to accede to the laws of the division of labor. Domestic work should be done by specialists.

In the modern world, moreover, with its intricate economic arrangements, our real loyalty must be to our work. The duty to work is paramount. Work is the primary social act if it is in keeping with the real needs of the economic order. Women as inefficient domestic workers or as wholly unproductive consumers were the relics of an outdated family system, remnants of an agrarian and feudal past, and wholly out of step with a democratic society geared to efficient production. Gilman was, in short, not primarily asking for women's individual rights but for their opportunity to participate as equals in the economic process, for that was where citizenship and its rewards and duties now rested.[36] To the extent that she was protesting against the conditions that prevented women from reaching their full economic potential, she was also pointing to the personal cost of their domestic slavery and stunted self-development. In this respect, in spite of her evolutionary historicism, she resorted also to a more traditional individualism.

Veblen evidently approved of Gilman's aspirations. In his celebrated book, *The Theory of the Leisure Class,* he showed an unusual degree of interest in and understanding of the enforced idleness against which well-to-do women were beginning to assert themselves. But he made a more negative argument than Gilman's, less for labor than against the atavism of the idle rich, the aristocrats so excoriated by earlier democrats. Veblen was less concerned to get work for those who needed it than he was to expose the primitive social habits of the leisure classes. Their crime was to evade industrial occupation in favor of "exploit," like sports, or other useless and highly damaging activities, such as religious observance, government, and war. Against them stands the "instinct of workmanship," to which we owe all that is best in productive and cooperative society. The difficulty is that it may not be a match for the leisurely values of the rich and their aversion to all useful employment.

Unlike Gilman, Veblen had no interest at all in the personal value of work for the unemployed individual. Nor did he belabor the idle rich as exploiters and oppressors. He was simply a very orthodox Jacksonian in his polemics against the unproductive rich.[37] He lacked their optimism, their faith in progress, but he shared their indignation. It was an outrage that had, however, lost some of its significance. Why should one mourn, as Veblen did, the passing of the spirit of workmanship if the creation of wealth for all was not affected? Why should the rich work? Who would benefit from it? Indeed, there was a strong movement to persuade the rich to be less busy and to devote themselves to charity, the arts, and the refinement of manners.[38] *Noblesse oblige* has, however, not been an overwhelmingly popular ideal in America, and Veblen was on solid native ground when he resorted to the rhetoric of the Jacksonians.

It seemed simply obvious, to Veblen at least, that inherited wealth and inherited gentility should no longer exercise their glamour. That they still did so was in no small measure due to the scholarly classes, who ape and promote the values of the leisured. They do this not out of any obvious need to fawn upon their patrons, but because they are prone to aristocratic nostalgia and romantic fantasies about the past. The mania for handicrafts, with all their inefficiency, was but a symptom of their general cultural lag. They also took innovation and efficiency to be bad form. The traces of feudal Europe, in short, were still visible in America.

Tom Paine's Norman banditti still had heirs all over America, in Veblen's view. The predatory instincts of the rich had not declined, so that in addition to looking down upon honest labor, these latter-day aristocrats were also extremely competitive. When they entered industry, as "captains," they retarded it with archaic devices of exploit and competition, when cooperation and workmanship were the real economic demands of an advanced industrial order. "Archaism" and "waste" were remnants of aristocratic virtue, and America could ill afford them.[39]

It is not always easy to understand why Veblen was so angry. If the idle classes were mere leftovers from an earlier stage of civilization, history was bound to sweep them away, and often he seemed to suggest just that. If they retarded progress, then they were, to be sure, a genuine obstacle, but one that could and would be removed by social legislation. Veblen did not appear to think such an outcome likely, as it indeed was not. Finally, and most plausibly, his was the voice of a simple moral protest against the fact that in republican, hard-working, industrial America there should still be so much aristocratic disdain for productive work.[40]

Infuriating as these primitive survivals were, it was no longer possible to argue that universal productivity as such was a collective good because it would raise

everyone's standard of living. Nor was it psychologically obvious that the spirit of workmanship was either as common or as powerful as Veblen took it to be,
or that it would have all those beneficent public consequences that he ascribed to it. Sheer labor is not workmanship. The Progressive reformers who continued
to preach the dignity of work did so for more plausible
reasons. They claimed that to remain competitive in a
world market, America needed self-reliant, educated,
and respected workers. And like Locke before them,
they thought that teaching manual skills and cookery
to middle-class pupils in school would contribute to
creating the appropriate ethos in an increasingly class-
differentiated America. That was not, however, Veblen's case. To the extent that he made an argument at
all, it was that the idle were out of step with history.
Perhaps the most interesting thing about his famous
book is the acute anxiety that idleness aroused in its
author. No contemporary advocate of workfare has
expressed this uneasiness with greater intensity. Only
the groups that inspire these fears and animadversion
have altered.

Most labor historians have confirmed the truth of
what was being said about industrial labor as soon as it
became prevalent in the United States. Workers disliked their work and did it solely for the sake of their
earnings. The discontent of people who do gainful
work solely in order to consume is not a new phenomenon; it is the permanent condition of industrial work.
It should, however, not surprise students of American

culture that the work ethic remains perfectly intact among these contrary impulses. The fear of unemployment has simply worked to reinforce the realization that only earning offers citizens their standing. The fears originally inspired by slavery, laced by racism and resentment of idleness at the top, were enhanced by the fear of being fired. The result is not perhaps a coherent ideology, but it is certainly an intelligible one. Not to work is not to earn, and without one's earnings one is "nobody."

Historical accretions have thus produced a mixed set of beliefs. The conviction that it is a duty to earn, that one can get ahead by one's own efforts, and that opportunities are open to those who seek them out, nestles beside the knowledge that unemployment is generally not the fault of the worker but of the economy as a whole. Job satisfaction is low, but no one enjoys being out of work, and even the poor on welfare profess to prefer work to idleness. If there are any idle rich, they certainly do not flaunt their wasteful lives, and when they do they are not admired by the rest of the wealthy. Sport may be as atavistic an activity as Veblen thought, but its pleasures are not class-specific.

Both the dignity of work and the public obligation to work are almost universally preached. Seventy-five percent of the American public think that there is something wrong with not wanting to work. A good citizen is an earner, because independence is the indelibly necessary quality of genuine, democratic citizenship. But few people blame either the poor or the system for poverty and unemployment. They are just facts of life, like the weather. Does this mishmash of social values and the realities of industrial society merely reveal that Americans are massively confused in their attitudes to earning?[41] Perhaps that is the case, but it may be more instructive to ask whether these apparently incoherent views do not express real social experiences. Surely it is possible that people who do not enjoy work may find unemployment even worse, and not only because of lowered income. The unemployed may feel that they have been disgraced for no particular fault of their own, and that they have become less than citizens. You can think the boss is a slave-driver, but you may feel more like a real slave when you are unemployed. And there is nothing illusory about these experiences. You have been expelled from civil society, reduced to second-class citizenship, a condition rendered all the more galling for white workers because it is associated with the normal lot of black people. For the latter, it is a doubling of unjust burdens.

The group to whom both these views make perfect sense are the unemployed, that is, people who have lost their jobs and who are looking for work. Unemployment is itself a very complex notion, implying both freedom and dependence. A slave cannot be unemployed or dismissed, though he may be used inefficiently. The free worker, who sells his labor but not himself, is nevertheless dependent on others for work.[42] A democratic citizen is, however, supposed to be entirely his own man. That is why wage earning as a system, with its dependence upon employers, was from the first looked upon with suspicion and fear as a threat to republican citizenship in the last century. Not only does the wage earner have to rely on others for remunerated work, he can be dismissed at any moment and then faces the loss of standing that being unemployed brings with it. And this loss of one's social position is itself felt as a loss of competency, which is inevitably enhanced when the unemployed person must seek help from others. Even finding a new job involves such experiences. In the best of the studies of unemployed men during the Great Depression, we thus find that the loss of independence was keenly felt. It might be argued that to have no work hardly resembles slavery, whose victims worked only too incessantly. The issue is not labor as such, but earning and the independence it confers. The slave is degraded not because he has to work—everyone should do that—but because he is kept rather than remunerated.

Few of the unemployed workers of the Great Depression claimed that they had liked their jobs. They missed the paycheck and the companionship of their fellow workers, but not their bosses or foremen. Nevertheless, they knew that to have a decent job, to be a producer and a good provider, was the sole ground of their social standing, and they certainly understood what it meant to lose that. They hated being unemployed. "What's life like without a job? You are nobody." When the Depression began this feeling was particularly humiliating, because it was not until about 1933 that the public finally grasped that unemployment was a national calamity, not the fault of the individual worker. Even so, in many cases the unemployed worker lost his family's respect and that of those around him. To accept relief, private or public, was painful, and many tried to rationalize it by recalling that they were veterans, or had paid taxes and contributed to charity in better times. The vast majority preferred WPA and work-relief to what were regarded as handouts.[43]

These attitudes are far from dead, and they survive especially strongly among the most successful children of these hard-pressed blue-collar workers.[44] It may well be that the sheer fear of unemployment, rather than any views about work itself, has come to sustain the work ethic and the ideal of the earning citizen. It is certainly not Veblen's instinct of workmanship, nor any noticeable contentment with work as such, that has kept the work ethic alive in an impersonal economy. Jacksonian ideology in contemporary America has attached itself not to the rights of the worker who demands respect in addition to an honest day's wage for an honest day's work, but to the unemployed. They want to work so that they can reclaim their citizenship as well as their paycheck. Who wants to be "nothing?"

The unemployed no longer feel guilty as they did

during the Great Depression, but independence has not lost its worth in their eyes. They prefer unemployment benefits from the government to private or family help, precisely because the former is impersonal and a right, and as such has no strings attached. There is much, however, that has remained constant. Unemployed Americans do not lose their faith in the American Dream, and they do not translate their personal economic troubles into political action. What they fear is welfare dependence, which has become the new focus of Jacksonian fears.[45] The locus of ideological conflict has, however, shifted from a struggle between workers and aristocrats to a quarrel between ideologically divided governing parties. One side accuses its opponents of being a parentalistic elite who want to eliminate poverty by paralyzing the poor. The second group charges the other side with being harsh populist achievers who blame the victims unfairly, and who in disregard of actual conditions and needs simply want to put everyone to work for a tiny wage and to no good end. What is really astonishing is the degree of agreement between these critics and defenders of welfare. Independence, exchanging the welfare check for a paycheck, is what both sides hope for. All want to make good citizens out of the "underclass" by getting them a job and making them, too, earning members of society.[46]

More than either side would admit, they are all still caught up in the Jacksonian web of ideas. The defender of the helpless poor wants to protect them against an army of predatory aristocrats who are denying them their rights and sustenance. The poor are social victims who are being denied racial equality, opportunities for decent work and education, and access to normal public goods. If more were done for them, they too would become upstanding laborers. The opposing party of individual effort, like Frederick Douglass, hopes that the government will do nothing more than ensure fair play for all. Anyone who truly wants to work, they argue, can find employment, and with it will come standing and self-respect. Both parties deeply believe in self-discipline, in independence, in work as the primary source of all value and all dignity, and in the ideal of a society of self-supporting democratic citizens. Each one sees the other as a threat to democracy and to the values of work and independence which they so profoundly share.

These survivals from the Jacksonian past color attitudes to welfare in obvious ways. The welfare recipients who are told that they must work at whatever job is available see the specter of slavery and indentured servitude come to haunt them again, returned from a not so distant past. And the persistence of racism makes that fear plausible. To those who want to see workfare made compulsory, the idle poor are no longer citizens. They have forfeited their claim to civic equality and are well on their way to behaving like unemployed slaves, kept consumers who do not produce. It is not claimed by either side that the work to be performed is likely to be socially useful or personally satisfying or well-paid. Workfare has nothing to do with economics. It is about citizenship, and whether able-bodied adults who do not earn anything actively can be regarded as full citizens. If they are not, may they not, as is now often the case, be treated with that mixture of parentalism and contempt that has always been reserved for the dependent classes? They are not citizens of civil society, and they are not accepted as such.[47] Unlike the unemployed, they are not trying to reestablish their standing, for they generally had none to lose in the first place.[48] What workfare is expected to achieve is to get them to maintain acceptable standards of civic conduct.

In many ways earning is like voting. Almost one-half of the voting-age population does not vote, though they would certainly resent disenfranchisement. With the exception of those lucky few who have a vocation for their work, or at least a sense of workmanship, Americans labor in order to be able to spend their wages. It is obviously ridiculous to speak of work as if it were an undifferentiated activity.[49] When they cease to earn, however, whatever the character of their work, Americans lose their standing in their communities. It is irrational and unfair, but it is a fundamental fact of life constituted of enduring and deeply entrenched social beliefs. They are not the best possible public values, nor do I wish to suggest that their being shared improves them in any way or endows them with any moral worth.[50] Above all, I do not mean to say that we should abstain from criticizing these habits of mind, simply because they are so old and so deeply entrenched. Nothing could be more absurd than the imputation that the critics of common and ancient ideologies are in some way contemptuous of their fellow-citizens and arrogant when they challenge them. To reveal the unfulfilled promises of traditional ideologies is certainly not the only significant form of social criticism, nor is it usually the most appropriate. I have resorted to it here only because I think it important to recall not only the antiquity and continuing prevalence and relevance of the Jacksonian faith, but also the fact that it creates a presumption of a right to work as an element of American citizenship, and that this ought to be recognized.

By the right to work I do not, of course, mean to endorse the anti-union legislation that prohibits closed shops, but rather the comprehensive commitment to providing opportunities for work to earn a living wage for all who need and demand it. It may not be a constitutional right or one that the courts should enforce, but it should be a presumption guiding our policies. Instead of being regarded as just one interest among others, it ought to enjoy the primacy that a right may claim in any conflict of political priorities.[51] In a polity of interest and rights-claiming individuals, only those who act on their own behalf and are recognized as competent in civil and political society can count as full citizens. If they lack the identifying marks of citizenship, they must fall into a proscribed category. With all these considerations in mind, there are

good reasons for claiming that there is a right to remunerated work in America.

The case against the right to work is not insignificant. There is no such self-evident moral right, and it
is not an enforceable legal one, it is said. Moreover,
self-respect is too vague and too subjective a state of
mind to be the ground for any public policy.[52] Instead
of thinking about rights at all, one should think in
terms of general policies designed to eliminate unemployment and to raise the standard of living of the
poor. One can, however, concede most of these points
and still argue for a right to work in America. It would
be a right derived from the requirements of local citizenship, not a primary human right. As a jury trial is
drawn from the primary right to a fair trial, in Anglo-
American legal practice, so earning is implicit in equal
American citizenship.[53] As such it must be entirely
separated from relief, now misnamed welfare, which
is based on need, however that may be estimated.
Relief should ideally be recognized as a basic service
due both to those who are and to those who are not
earners, at any given moment. We ought to learn to
think of it in the same terms as public roads and sanita-
tion, but we probably will not.

The right to earn should not be based on personal re-
sponses, such as loss of self-respect among the unemployed, but on the loss of public respect, the reduction
of standing and demotion to second-class citizenship,
to which the public ethos, overtly and traditionally,
condemns them. It is not a right to self-respect, but a

right not to be deprived of one's standing as a citizen, that is at stake here. And the minimal political obligation must be the creation of paying jobs geographically close to the unemployed and offering them a legally set minimum wage and the chance of advancement.[54] Like any right, the right to earn can be forfeited, but that does not render it worthless. And even if it is not feasible to enforce the right fully, the consciousness of the claim can have a political effect.

These reflections end my brief sketch of American democratic citizenship as standing. It is not meant to be a full account of all that citizenship is or might be, but only an attempt to illuminate two of its most elementary and essential components: voting and earning, as they have emerged out of the stress of inherited inequalities, especially the remnants of black chattel slavery, in a society committed to political equality and to the principle of inclusion.

NOTES

INDEX

NOTES

INTRODUCTION

1. Richard P. Coleman and Lee Rainwater, *Social Standing in America* (New York: Basic Books, 1978), passim.
2. Kirk H. Porter, *A History of Suffrage in the United States* (Chicago: University of Chicago Press, 1918), pp. 112–134. Leon E. Aylesworth, "The Passing of Alien Suffrage," *American Political Science Review*, 25 (1931), 114–116.
3. Aristotle, *The Politics,* trans. and ed. Carns Lord (Chicago: University of Chicago Press, 1985), bk. 3, chap. 4, 1276b–1277b, pp. 90–92.
4. Ibid., bk. 3, chap. 3, 1276a–1277b, pp. 89–90.
5. As an example of the right way to discuss citizenship I would cite Dennis F. Thompson, *The Democratic Citizen* (Cambridge: Cambridge University Press, 1970), a model of how to integrate political theory and political science.
6. See Cass R. Sunstein, "Beyond the Republican Revival," *Yale Law Journal,* 97 (1988), 1539–1590, for an example of how remote from anything concrete even the best of the legalistic republicanism now is.
7. See Kay Lehman Schlozman and Sidney Verba, *Insult to Injury* (Cambridge, Mass.: Harvard University Press, 1979), pp. 103–138, 346–351, for an account of its hold even on the unemployed and working poor.
8. Hannah Arendt, "What Is Authority?" in *Between Past and Future* (New York: Viking, 1961), pp. 91–141.
9. Austin Ranney, "Theory" and "United States of America," in *Referendums,* ed. David Butler and Austin Ranney (Washington, D.C.: American Enterprise Institute, 1978), pp. 23–37, 67–86.

10. See Benjamin Barber, *Strong Democracy: Participatory Politics for a New Age* (Berkeley: University of California Press, 1984), for a sense of how transforming participatory democracy would have to be.

11. For a much-needed corrective, see Gordon Wood, "The Fundamentalists and the Constitution," *New York Review of Books,* vol. 35, no. 2 (1988), pp. 33–40.

12. Louis Hartz, *The Liberal Tradition in America* (New York: Harcourt, Brace, 1954), and Samuel P. Huntington, *American Politics: The Promise of Disharmony* (Cambridge, Mass.: Harvard University Press, 1981). I have been very careful not to follow their tendency to even out the discontinuities in America's past, and especially to exaggerate American liberalism. In this I have been particularly helped by Rogers M. Smith, "The 'American Creed' and American Identity: The Limits of Liberal Citizenship in the United States," *Western Political Quarterly,* 41 (1988), 225–251, and "One United People: Second Class Female Citizenship and the American Quest for Community," *Yale Journal of Law and the Humanities,* 1 (1989), 229–293.

13. James H. Kettner, *The Development of American Citizenship, 1608–1870* (Chapel Hill: University of North Carolina Press, 1978), p. 288.

14. Porter, *A History of Suffrage,* pp. 109–111.

15. In his *New York Times* column of June 19, 1970, James Reston expressed dismay and surprise at the lack of interest that politically active young people showed toward the lowering of the voting age. There was in fact very little press attention at the time, nor have scholars found the amendment fascinating. I have relied entirely on about a dozen brief stories in the *New York Times;* see especially the issues of March 24, 1971, and July 1, 1971.

16. Charles E. Merriam, *American Political Ideas: 1865–1917* (New York: Augustus M. Kelley, 1969), pp. 94–96.

17. Jane J. Mansbridge, *Why We Lost the ERA* (Chicago: University of Chicago Press, 1986), p. 104.

18. Merriam, *American Political Ideas,* pp. 80–81.

19. Marcus Cunliffe, *Chattel Slavery and Wage Slavery* (Athens, Ga.: University of Georgia Press, 1979), pp. 1–31.

20. David Montgomery, *Beyond Equality: Labor and the Radical Republicans, 1862–1872* (New York: Random House, 1967), pp. 123–124.

21. Ibid., p. 251.

ONE: VOTING

1. Quoted in Kenneth L. Karst, *Belonging to America* (New Haven, Conn.: Yale University Press, 1989), p. 94.

2. *The Federalist Papers,* ed. Clinton Rossiter (New York: New American Library, 1961), no. 61, p. 373.

3. Charles E. Merriam and Harold F. Gosnell, *Non-Voting* (Chicago: University of Chicago Press, 1924), pp. 1–2.

4. Frances Fox Piven and Richard A. Cloward, *Why Americans Don't Vote* (New York: Pantheon, 1989).

5. Kim Ezra Schienbaum, *Beyond the Electoral Connection* (Philadelphia: University of Pennsylvania Press, 1984), pp. 10, 126.

6. Raymond E. Wolfinger and Steven J. Rosenstone, *Who Votes?* (New Haven, Conn.: Yale University Press, 1980), pp. 7–8.

7. Aristotle, *The Politics,* bk. 1, chaps. 3–13, 1253b–1260a, pp. 38–54; bk. 7, chaps. 1–15, 1323a–1334b, pp. 197–223.

8. Most notably Hannah Arendt, *The Human Condition* (Chicago: University of Chicago Press, 1958).

9. See especially Quentin Skinner, *Machiavelli* (Oxford: Oxford University Press, 1981).

10. Thomas Hobbes, *De Cive,* ed. Sterling P. Lamprecht (New York: Appleton-Century-Crofts, 1949), pp. 86, 114–115, 119–120.

11. Jean Bodin, *The Six Bookes of the Commonwealth,* ed. K. D. McRae (Cambridge, Mass.: Harvard University Press, 1962), bk. 1, chap. 6, pp. 46–69.

12. Kettner, *The Development of American Citizenship,* pp. 316–317.

13. Jean Jacques Rousseau, *Emile,* in *Oeuvres Complètes* (Paris: Pléiade, 1969), p. 249; *Contrat Social,* ibid., vol. 3, bk. 1, chaps.

6, 7, 8; bk. 2, chaps. 4, 5, 11; bk. 3, chaps. 9, 14, 15; bk. 4, chaps. 2, 3. *Constitution pour la Corse,* ibid., p. 919. (I cite the chapters only for the *Social Contract* because so many editions of it are in common use.)

14. In the one direct mention of Rousseau in the pamphlet literature of 1787, his argument against representation is significantly cited with approval. See "Essay by a Newport Man" in *The Complete Anti-Federalist,* ed. Herbert J. Storing (Chicago: University of Chicago Press, 1981), vol. 4, pp. 250–254.

15. Quoted in Keith Baker, *Condorcet* (Chicago: University of Chicago Press, 1975), p. 208.

16. Quoted in Chilton Williamson, *American Suffrage from Property to Democracy, 1760–1860* (Princeton, N.J.: Princeton University Press, 1960), p. 11.

17. *The Federalist,* no. 35, pp. 214–217.

18. Hobbes, *De Cive,* p. 110.

19. Bernard Bailyn, *The Ideological Origins of the American Revolution* (Cambridge, Mass.: Harvard University Press, 1967); Edmund S. Morgan, *American Slavery, American Freedom* (New York: Norton, 1975); Abbot E. Smith, *Colonists in Bondage: White Servitude and Convict Labor in America, 1607–1776* (New York: Norton, 1971).

20. Edmund Burke, "Speech on Conciliation with America," in *Works* (Boston: Little, Brown, 1881), vol. 2, pp. 123–124.

21. Morgan, *American Slavery, American Freedom,* p. 376.

22. James Otis, *The Rights of the British Colonies Asserted and Proved* (1764), in *Tracts of the American Revolution: 1763–1776,* ed. Merrill Jensen (Indianapolis: Bobbs-Merrill, 1967), pp. 20–40.

23. I owe this apt phrase to George Kateb.

24. Donald L. Robinson, *Slavery in the Structure of American Politics, 1765–1820* (New York: Harcourt, Brace, Jovanovich, 1971), pp. 64–80.

25. See Daniel Dulany, *Considerations on the Propriety of Imposing Taxes in the British Colonies for the Purpose of Raising a Revenue, by Act of Parliament* (1765), in Jensen, *Tracts,* pp. 95–107.

26. Steven F. Lawson, *Black Ballots: Voting Rights in the South, 1944–1969* (New York: Columbia University Press, 1976), p. 286.

27. "The Putney Debates," in *Divine Right and Democracy*, ed. David Wootton (Harmondsworth, England: Penguin, 1986), pp. 285–317.

28. Williamson, *American Suffrage*, p. 133.

29. Wootton, ed., *Divine Right and Democracy*, p. 286.

30. Merrill D. Peterson, ed., *Democracy, Liberty, and Property: The State Constitutional Conventions of the 1820's* (Indianapolis: Bobbs-Merrill, 1966), p. 61.

31. Ibid., p. 383.

32. Ibid., pp. 408–409.

33. Ibid., pp. 335–336.

34. Ibid., pp. 399–400.

35. Ibid., pp. 194–196.

36. *The Life and Writings of Frederick Douglass*, vol. 4, ed. Philip S. Foner (New York: International Publishers, 1955), p. 167.

37. Ibid., p. 27.

38. Ibid., pp. 162–163.

39. Eric Foner, *Reconstruction* (New York: Harper and Row, 1988), pp. 8–9.

40. William Gillette, *The Right to Vote: Politics and the Passage of the Fifteenth Amendment* (Baltimore: Johns Hopkins University Press, 1965), p. 40.

41. See Rayford W. Logan, ed., *What the Negro Wants* (Chapel Hill: University of North Carolina Press, 1944), generally and especially the essays of Charles H. Wesley and Mary McLeod Bethune. Lawson, *Black Ballots*, p. 65.

42. Foner, ed., *Life and Writings of Frederick Douglass*, p. 509.

43. Ibid., p. 158.

44. Gillette, *The Right to Vote*, p. 162. James M. McPherson, *The Struggle for Equality* (Princeton, N.J.: Princeton University Press, 1964), p. 240.

45. Gillette, *The Right to Vote*, pp. 87–88.

46. Foner, *Reconstruction*, pp. 278–279.
47. Sidney Verba and Norman H. Nie, *Participation in America* (New York: Harper and Row, 1972), pp. 106–114, 341–342.
48. Quoted in Lawson, *Black Ballots*, pp. 16–17.
49. Foner, ed., *Life and Writings of Frederick Douglass*, pp. 159–160.
50. Ellen Carol Du Bois, *Feminism and Suffrage* (Ithaca, N.Y.: Cornell University Press, 1978), p. 59.
51. *Minor v. Happersett*, 21 Wall. 162, 1874.
52. Quoted in Aileen S. Kraditor, *The Ideas of the Women's Suffrage Movement, 1890–1920* (New York: Anchor Books, 1971), pp. 40–41.
53. Elizabeth Cady Stanton, "Women as Patriots," in *Reminiscences*, ed. Theodore Stanton and Harriot Stanton Black (New York: Harper and Brothers, 1922), pp. 193–203.
54. Linda K. Kerber, *Women of the Republic: Intellect and Ideology in Revolutionary America* (Chapel Hill: University of North Carolina Press, 1980), pp. 283–288.
55. Du Bois, *Feminism and Suffrage*, p. 178.

TWO: EARNING

1. *The Philosophy of Right*, trans. T. M. Knox (Oxford: Oxford University Press, 1942), secs. 182–256.
2. Robert E. Lane, "Government and Self Esteem," *Political Theory*, 10 (1982), 5–31.
3. Robert E. Wiebe, *The Opening of American Society* (New York: Vintage Books, 1985), pp. 264–290.
4. Michel Chevalier, *Society, Manners, and Politics in the United States* (1839) (New York: Augustus M. Kelley, 1966), pp. 296–304. I shall use this work rather more than Tocqueville's celebrated book, because in many ways Chevalier was a more direct and undidactic observer.
5. Alexis de Tocqueville, *Democracy in America*, trans. George Lawrence (New York: Doubleday, 1969), vol. 11, bk. 2, chap. 18, p. 550.

6. One need only look at the plates on the crafts in the *Encyclopédie* and at some of Goya's paintings to recognize the intensity of the aspiration to dignify work in the Enlightenment.

7. John Garraty, *Unemployment in History* (New York: Harper and Row, 1978), pp. 38–42.

8. *Some Thoughts Concerning Education*, in *Works* (London: 1823), vol. 9, secs. 202–212.

9. Max Weber, *The Protestant Ethic and the Spirit of Capitalism*, trans. Talcott Parsons (London: Allen and Unwin, 1948), pp. 50–57.

10. Esmond Wright, *Franklin of Philadelphia* (Cambridge, Mass.: Harvard University Press, 1986), p. 358.

11. "Father Abraham's Speech," in *The Complete Poor Richard's Almanacks* (Boston: Imprint Society, 1970), vol. 2, p. 14.

12. Andrew Jackson, "A Political Testament," in *Social Theories of Jacksonian Democracy,* ed. Joseph L. Blau (Indianapolis: Bobbs-Merrill, 1954), pp. 1–20.

13. Ralph Waldo Emerson, "The Young American," in *Essays and Lectures* (New York: The Library of America, 1983), pp. 213–230.

14. William Leggett, "Democratic Editorials," in *Social Theories,* ed. Blau, pp. 66–88.

15. Stephen Simpson, "Political Economy and the Workers," in *Social Theories,* ed. Blau, pp. 137–162.

16. Chevalier, *Society, Manners, and Politics,* pp. 205–206, 282–288.

17. Wiebe, *Opening of American Society,* p. 286.

18. John Ashford, *"Agrarians" and "Aristocrats"* (Cambridge: Cambridge University Press, 1987), p. 91 and passim.

19. Herbert G. Gutman, *Work, Culture, and Society in Industrializing America* (New York: Vintage Books, 1977), p. 51.

20. Ely Moore, "On Labor Unions," in *Social Theories,* ed. Blau, pp. 289–300.

21. Wiebe, *Opening of American Society,* p. 165.

22. Stephen Simpson, in *Social Theories,* ed. Blau, pp. 142–146.

23. "The Federal Farmer," in *The Complete Anti-Federalist,* ed. Herbert J. Storing (Chicago: University of Chicago Press, 1981), vol. 2, p. 236. *Notes on the State of Virginia,* in *The Portable Thomas Jefferson,* ed. Merrill D. Peterson (New York: Viking Press, 1975), pp. 214–215.

24. This list and more appear in the best of all abolitionist tracts, Richard Hildreth's *Despotism in America* (New York: Augustus Kelley, 1970), pp. 142–168.

25. Joseph Dorfman, *The Economic Mind in American Civilization, 1606–1865* (New York: Viking Press, 1946), pp. 666–667.

26. Daniel Rodgers, *The Work Ethic in Industrial America, 1850–1920* (Chicago: University of Chicago Press, 1978), pp. 30–31 and passim.

27. Eric Foner, *Free Soil, Free Labor, Free Men* (New York: Oxford University Press, 1970), pp. 11, 15–16, 40–72, 296, and passim.

28. James M. McPherson, *Battle Cry of Freedom* (New York: Oxford University Press, 1988), pp. 195–198.

29. Abraham Lincoln, "Agriculture: Annual Address before the Wisconsin Agricultural Society, at Milwaukee, Wisconsin. September 30, 1859" and "Annual Message to Congress. December 3, 1861," in *Speeches and Writings,* ed. Roy P. Basler (Cleveland: World, 1946), pp. 493–504 and 616–635.

30. Foner, *Reconstruction,* pp. 102–110.

31. Foner, ed., *Life and Writings of Frederick Douglass,* vol. 4, pp. 271–272.

32. Foner, *Reconstruction,* pp. 114–115.

33. W. E. B. Du Bois, *The Souls of Black Folk* (New York: New American Library, 1982), p. 198.

34. John Stuart Mill, *On the Subjection of Women* (London: Everyman's Library, 1929), p. 248.

35. Rodgers, *Work Ethic,* pp. 30–93.

36. Charlotte Perkins Gilman, *Women and Economics* (New York: Harper and Row, 1966), pp. 17, 22, 93–94, 117–118, 152, 211, 218, 245–247, 276–279, 333.

37. David Riesman, *Thorstein Veblen* (New York: Seabury Press,

1960), p. 91. Theodor W. Adorno, "Veblen's Attack on Culture," in *Prisms* (Cambridge, Mass.: MIT Press, 1981), pp. 75–94.

38. Rodgers, *Work Ethic,* pp. 94–124.

39. Thorstein Veblen, *The Theory of the Leisure Class* (New York: New American Library, 1953), pp. 21, 29, 64, 75–76, 87, 116–117, 138, 158, 256.

40. This is not a full account of the works of Veblen, but only of his early and most famous book. He continued to change and develop his views throughout his life, but his fame rests largely on *The Theory of the Leisure Class.*

41. Herbert McClosky and John Zaller, *The American Ethos* (Cambridge, Mass.: Harvard University Press, 1984), passim.

42. Garraty, *Unemployment in History,* pp. 5–6.

43. E. W. Bakke, *The Unemployed Worker* (New Haven, Conn.: Yale University Press, 1940), pp. 39, 84, 87–89, 316–328. Mirra Komarovsky, *The Unemployed Worker and His Family* (New York: Dryden Press, 1940), passim. Schlozman and Verba, *Insult to Injury,* pp. 4–84.

44. When the sons of blue-collar families who were engineers and scientists lost their jobs in the Boston high-tech industries in the 1970s, they were often too ashamed to tell their friends and neighbors. Paula Goldman Leventman, *Professionals out of Work* (New York: Free Press, 1981), passim.

45. Schlozman and Verba, *Insult to Injury.*

46. See, for example, these typical and serious pro-welfare writings: Sheldon Danziger, "Fighting Poverty and Reducing Welfare Dependency," in *Welfare Policy for the 1990s,* ed. David T. Ellwood (Cambridge, Mass.: Harvard University Press, 1989), pp. 41–69, and David T. Ellwood, *Poor Support* (New York: Basic Books, 1988), pp. 3–44.

47. For the most perfect account of these views see Lawrence M. Mead, *Beyond Entitlement* (New York: Free Press, 1986), pp. 12–13, 41–45, 211–212, 238.

48. Their negative experiences in the workplace may in fact account for their passivity, at least according to Leonard Good-

man, *Do the Poor Want to Work?* (Washington, D.C.: The Brookings Institution, 1972), pp. 112–118.

49. Gregory E. Pence, "Towards a Theory of Work," *Philosophical Forum,* 10 (1978–79), 306–311.

50. I emphasize this point because I do not want this argument to be identified in any way with Michael Walzer's endorsement of shared values as a general ethical justification of social practices. Nothing in these essays should be taken as support for the leading notions of his *Spheres of Justice* (New York: Basic Books, 1983).

51. The analogy to "welfare rights" as T. H. Marshall discusses them is quite intentionally close. They are not legally binding, but they are implied in the level of subsistence that the standing of a citizen requires. See T. H. Marshall, *The Right to Welfare and Other Essays* (New York: Free Press, 1981), pp. 11, 83–103.

52. Jon Elster, "Is There (or Should There Be) a Right to Work?" in *Democracy and the Welfare State,* ed. Amy Gutmann (Princeton, N.J.: Princeton University Press, 1988), pp. 53–78.

53. James W. Nickel, "Is There a Human Right to Employment?" *Philosophical Forum,* 10 (1978–79), 149–170.

54. See William Julius Wilson, *The Truly Disadvantaged* (Chicago: University of Chicago Press, 1987), pp. 159–163.

INDEX

Abolitionism, 7, 41, 54, 55, 57, 79, 84, 85. *See also* Slavery
Active participant citizen, 3, 5–7, 10, 29–31
American exceptionalism, 28
American Revolution, 15, 39–43, 70–71
Anthony, Susan, 60
Aristocracy, 64–67; disdain for work in, 2, 69–70, 74–75, 79, 85, 88–91; Constitutional proscription of, 61, 64, 85; workers' disdain of, 66, 74–75, 82, 83, 85–91; undue political influence of, 72–74
Aristotle: citizenship in, 6, 8, 12, 29–31, 33; on goodness, 6–7; exclusionism of, 29

Bank of the United States, 66
Bethune, Mary McLeod, 109n41
Blacks. *See* Black suffrage; Slavery
Blackstone, Sir William, 37
Black suffrage: racist disenfranchisement of blacks, 44, 51–52, 61; use of civic virtue in, 52–53; use of natural rights in, 53–57. *See also* Voting
Bodin, Jean, 34, 39; naturalization in, 32–33
Brownson, Orestes, 80
Burke, Edmund, 40

Chevalier, Michel, 110n4
Citizenship: and earning, 1–2, 3, 8, 15–17, 19–22, 64–68, 80–84, 92–97; as empowerment and agency, 2, 54–55; as social standing, 2–3, 14, 27, 28, 52–54, 56–57, 59–60, 63, 92–94, 101; and voting, 2–3, 45–46, 49–50, 55–56, 64, 66; as active participation, 3, 5–7, 10, 29–31; as ideal republican, 3, 10–13, 34–36, 65–67; as nationality, 3–5, 8–9, 10; in Aristotle, 6, 8, 12, 29–31, 33; women excluded from, 7–8, 16–17, 29, 34–35, 57–61; slaves excluded from, 14, 16–17, 19–22, 29, 36–37, 47–52, 64, 66; property qualification for, 16, 35–36, 37, 43, 44–46, 47, 49–51, 58; equal distribution of, 16–17, 30, 33; in Hobbes, 32–33, 39; in Bodin, 32–33, 39; in Rousseau, 34; in Turgot, 36; in Locke, 36–37; and self-ownership, 36–37. *See also* Active participant citizen; Citizen-proprietor; Citizen-soldier; Citizen-subject; Earning; Good citizen; Native citizen; Republican citizen; Voting; Work
Citizen-proprietor, 36–37, 82
Citizen-soldier, 31, 48, 51, 53, 59
Citizen-subject, 33–34, 35

Civic virtue, 28, 31, 65–66; and
voting, 38–39, 50, 51; and
women's suffrage, 59–60. See
also Republican citizen
Civil society, 39, 63, 72, 93
Civil standing. See Social standing
Civil War, 10, 16, 20, 22, 46, 48,
52, 82, 86
Cleveland Leader, 76
Constitution, United States, 10,
15–16, 61, 64; Fourteenth
Amendment, 15; Fifteenth
Amendment, 53, 57; Twenty-
sixth Amendment, 18
Cromwell, Oliver, 44, 46

Daughters of the American Revolution, 69
Declaration of Independence, 13,
37, 44, 60, 72, 75
Democracy: and heredity, 61; and
work, 75–79. See also Participatory democracy; Representative
democracy
Direct democracy. See Participatory
democracy
Discrimination, 13–14
Douglass, Frederick, 56–57, 58, 97;
on voting, 52–54; on work, 83–
84
Dred Scott decision, 33, 58
Du Bois, W. E. B., 56, 84

Earning: and citizenship, 1–2, 3, 8,
15–17, 19–22, 64–68, 80–84, 92–
97; and work, 1–2, 67–68, 77,
81–83, 85–86, 91–93; and
women, 19–20, 84–88; and voting, 63–67, 98–99; and economic
independence, 67–68, 81–83, 85,

94. See also Unemployment;
Work
Economic independence, 21, 28,
37, 64–65, 67–68, 81–83, 85; and
. honor, 68; and unemployment,
94–97. See also Unemployment;
Work
Education, public, 54, 68, 75–77,
79, 97
Egalitarianism. See Equal political
rights
Emancipation Proclamation, 59
Emerson, Ralph Waldo, 73–74, 77
Enlightenment, 68, 111n6
Equal political rights: and exclusion, 1, 3, 13, 14–15, 16–17, 28–
30, 38; for women, 19–20, 57–
61; in Rousseau, 35; for white
men, 43–50, 66–67; for blacks,
52–57
Equal Rights Amendment, 19–20
Exclusionism: and equal political
rights, 1, 3, 13, 14–15, 16–17,
28–30, 38; racist, 4, 8, 13–14, 38,
51–52, 57–58, 79, 80, 82, 92, 97;
nativist, 4, 13–14, 38; sexist, 13–
14, 16–17, 27, 38, 46, 49, 57–61.
See also Nativism; Racism; Sexism

Fair trial, 33, 100
Feudalism, 73, 74
Fifteenth Amendment, 53, 57
Fitzhugh, George: Cannibals All, 80
Fourteenth Amendment, 15
France, 33
Franklin, Benjamin, 71–72
Freedmen, 16, 17; disenfranchise-
ment of, 51–55; enfranchisement
of, 55–57. See also Slavery

Freedom, 1, 40, 41. *See also* Economic independence; Slavery
Free Soil Party, 80

Garrison, William Lloyd, 21
Gender. *See* Suffrage; Women
Gilman, Charlotte Perkins, 86–87, 89
Good citizen, 3, 5–6; and good person, 6–8
Government: direct, 11; usefulness of, 70; and influence buying, 74. *See also* Participatory democracy; Representative democracy
Great Depression, 22, 94–95
Great Society, 62

Hamilton, Alexander, 25, 26, 39
Hand, Learned, 25
Hegel, G. W. F., 63
Hildreth, Richard: *Despotism in America*, 112n24
Hobbes, Thomas, 32–33, 34, 39
Honor, 68

Idle rich, 2, 70, 74–75, 79, 85, 88–91, 92. *See also* Aristocracy
Indentured servitude, 40. *See also* Slavery
Inequality: natural, 73, 74; artificial, 74, 77. *See also* Equal political rights
Ireton, Henry, 44–46, 53

Jackson, Andrew, 44, 46, 47, 73
Jacksonian democracy: abolition of property qualifications in, 46; racism in, 51–52, 79; disdain of aristocracy in, 66–67, 72–75; dig-

nity of work in, 75–76, 83–84, 85, 95–96; slavery in, 79, 84
Jacobins, 66
Jefferson, Thomas, 44, 47, 72, 79, 82
Johnson, Samuel (Dr.), 40

Kateb, George, 108n23
Kent, Chancellor, 50

Labor. *See* Earning; Slavery; Unemployment; Work
Labor theory of value, 67
Lee, Richard Henry, 79
Legal rights, 33
Leggett, William, 75
Liberalism, 13, 60, 106n12
Lincoln, Abraham, 7, 81–82
Literacy tests, 55. *See also* Voting
Locke, John, 91; citizenship in, 36–37; work in, 70
Lowell, Massachusetts, 76

Machiavelli, 31
Madison, James, 13; *The Federalist Papers*, 10, 65
Marshall, T. H., 114n51
Marxism, 27
Massachusetts, 16, 47, 76
Mechanical arts, 78. *See also* Work
Mill, John Stuart, 84
Monarchical absolutism, 32, 66
Money, 67–68. *See also* Earning; Unemployment; Work
Monopoly, 73, 75, 85
Montesquieu, 12
Morgan, Edmund, 40

Native-born Americans, 17
Native citizen, 3–5, 8–9, 10

Nativism, 4, 13–14, 38
Natural rights, 37–38, 86–87; and
    women's suffrage, 60–61
Nero, 32
New York Mechanics Society, 77
Noblesse oblige, 89

Otis, James, 41–42

Paine, Thomas, 73, 90
Parallelism, 67
Participatory democracy, 11, 30
Patriotism, 5. See also Civic virtue
Phillips, Wendell, 21, 54, 58
Political agency. See Citizenship;
    Equal political rights; Voting
Political rights. See Citizenship;
    Equal political rights; Voting
Poll taxes, 55
Poverty, 47, 97
Presidency, U.S., 74
Privilege: rejection of hereditary, 1,
    61; and citizenship, 33; voting as,
    58
Progressivism, 91
Property: as voting qualification,
    16, 36–37, 43, 44–46, 47, 49–51,
    58; disdain for, 78. See also Aris-
    tocracy
Protestantism, 71
Public standing. See Social standing
Puritanism, 70–71
Putney Debates, 44–46, 53

Race: and heredity, 61. See also
    Nativism; Racism
Racism, 4, 8, 38, 97; institutionaliz-
    ation of, 13–14; use of, for disen-
    franchisement, 44, 46, 51–52, 61;
    of early women's suffrage move-

ment, 57–58; of Jacksonian dem-
    ocrats, 79, 80; of workers, 82, 92
Rainborough, Colonel, 47
Reform Act, 47
Registration laws, 26. See also Vot-
    ing
Representation: equal, 16, 28, 38,
    42, 46–47; prestige of, 42; vir-
    tual, 42, 43; actual, 43
Representative democracy, 11–12,
    38, 65–66
Republican citizen: classical, 3, 10–
    13, 34–36; virtue of, 11–13;
    modern, 65–67
Republican party, 53–54, 59–60
Reston, James, 106n15
Rights, political. See Equal political
    rights
Right to work, 2–3, 65, 99–100;
    for women, 19–20; and slavery,
    19–22. See also Earning; Work
Rome, 10, 12
Rotarianism, 72
Rousseau, Jean-Jacques: citizenship
    in, 12, 34–36; women in, 34–35;
    equality of rights in, 35; voting
    in, 35–36

Scholarly classes, 89–90
Self-achievement, 1–2, 60, 68, 77
Self-employment, 64–65, 81–82
Self-ownership, 36
Self-respect, 63, 100
Sexism, 13–14, 38; use of, for dis-
    enfranchisement, 16–17, 27, 46,
    49, 57–61
Simpson, Stephen, 75
Slavery: and degradation of work,
    1–2, 79–84; abolitionists and, 7,
    41, 54, 55, 57, 79, 84, 85; institu-

tionalization of, 13–14; and exclusion of citizenship, 14, 16–17,
19–22, 29, 36–37; and voting,
16–17, 27, 35, 47–52; and social
standing, 16–17, 27, 41–42, 64,
66; use of, in gender equality debates, 19–20, 84–85; in Aristotle,
29–30; use of, in American Revolutionary debates, 39–43; and
liberal ideology, 40, 64; disgrace
of, 68, 87; and unemployment,
93
Smith, Rogers M., 106n12
Social Darwinism, 38, 60
Social independence. *See* Economic
independence
Social prestige, 42, 57
Social respect, 2, 67, 72, 76, 88–94,
98–101
Social standing: and work, 1–2, 67,
72, 76, 88–94, 98–101; and voting, 2, 27, 28, 52–54, 56–57, 59–
60; and citizenship, 2–3, 14, 63;
and slavery, 16–17, 27, 41–42,
66; and age, 19–20; and unemployment, 94–95
Sons of the American Revolution,
69
Sovereignty, 32, 35; and consent,
32–33
Stanton, Elizabeth Cady, 59–60
Stowe, Harriet Beecher: *Uncle
Tom's Cabin*, 84
Suffrage: for blacks, 19, 20, 51–57;
for women, 19–20, 57–61; for
white men, 43–50, 66. *See also*
Voting
Supreme Court, 9, 18

Taney, Roger Brooke, 16

Taxes: and citizenship, 33, 36–37;
and government size, 74
Technology, 78–79
Thompson, Dennis F., 105n5
Tocqueville, Alexis de, 68, 110n4
Turgot, Anne Robert Jacques, 36
Twain, Mark, 86
Twenty-sixth Amendment, 18,
106n15

Unemployment: shame of, 22, 93,
113n44; and earning, 91–92; and
slavery, 93; and social standing,
94–95; and independence, 94–97;
fear of, 95; and welfare, 97–98
Unions, 21–22

Veblen, Thorstein, 86, 88–91,
113n40; *The Theory of The Leisure Class*, 88
Vermont, 46
Vietnam war, 18
Virginia Convention, 48–49
Virtuous citizen. *See* Good citizen;
Republican citizen
Voluntary organizations, 31, 63
Voting: and social standing, 2, 27,
28, 52–54, 56–57, 59–60; and citizenship, 2–3, 45–46, 49–50, 55–
56, 64, 66; property qualification
for, 16, 37, 43, 44–46, 49–51, 58;
and slavery, 16–17, 27, 35, 47–
52; and women, 16–17, 27, 46,
49, 57–61; in teenagers, 17–19;
apathy toward, 17–19, 25–28,
106n15; natural right to, 27–28,
44, 45, 56–57, 60–61; in Rousseau, 35–36; and civic virtue, 38–
39, 51–52; racist disenfranchisement of, 44, 46, 52–57, 61; as

Voting (*cont.*)
  privilege, 50–51, 58; in Frederick
  Douglass, 52–54; as empowerment, 54–55; and earning, 63–
  67, 98–99
Voting Rights Act of 1965, 5

Wage labor. *See* Work
Walzer, Michael, 114n50
War of 1812, 46
Washington, Booker T., 20
Wealth, inherited. *See* Aristocracy
Weber, Max, 71
Welfare, 22, 97–98
Wesley, Charles H., 109n41
William the Conqueror, 73
Women: exclusion of, from citizen-
  ship, 7–8, 16–17, 29, 34–35, 57–
  61; and voting, 16–17, 19, 27,
  46, 49, 57–61; and earning, 19–
  20, 84–88; and slavery, 20, 84–
  85; in Aristotle, 29; in Rousseau,
  34–35
Women's suffrage: racism of early,
  57–58; and social standing, 58–
  59; use of civic virtue in, 59–60;
  use of natural rights in, 60–61

Work: and citizenship, 1–2, 3, 15–
  17, 19–22, 64–67, 92–97; and social standing, 1–2, 67, 72, 76,
  88–94, 98–101; and earning, 1–2,
  67–68, 77, 81–83, 85–86, 91–93;
  degradation of, and slavery, 1–2,
  79–84; dignity of, 2, 68–72, 75–
  79, 92, 96–97; aristocratic disdain
  for, 2, 69–70, 74–75, 79, 85, 88–
  91; and women, 19–20, 84–88;
  and independence, 21, 28, 37,
  64–65, 67–68, 81–83, 85, 94; and
  equal political rights, 63–67, 98–
  99; and disdain for aristocracy,
  66, 74–75, 82, 83, 85–91; and
  parallelism, 67; and public education, 75–79. *See also* Earning;
  Unemployment
Work ethic, 64, 71, 92
Workfare, 91, 97–98
Workmanship, 88, 89, 91
Works Progress Administration, 95
World War II, 53

Xenophobia, 4, 35

Yates, Richard, 55